**Editors**
Tracy Edmunds, M.A.
Sara Connolly
Heather Douglas

**Contributing Editor—Canada**
Jennifer Dorval

**Managing Editor**
Ina Massler Levin, M.A.

**Illustrator**
Sue Fullam

**Cover Artist**
Brenda DiAntonis

**Art Production Manager**
Kevin Barnes

**Art Coordinator**
Renée Christine Yates

**Imaging**
Rosa C. See
Nathan P. Rivera

***Publisher***
*Mary D. Smith, M.S. Ed.*

**Author**

Susan Mackey Collins, M.Ed.



***Teacher Created Resources, Inc.***
6421 Industry Way
Westminster, CA 92683
www.teachercreated.com
**ISBN: 978-1-4206-2743-5**

Made in U.S.A.

# Table of Contents



 

# Introduction

The wealth of knowledge a person gains throughout his or her lifetime is impossible to measure, and it will certainly vary from person to person. However, regardless of the scope of knowledge, the foundation for all learning remains a constant. All that we know and think throughout our lifetimes is based upon fundamentals, and these fundamentals are the basic skills upon which all learning develops. *Mastering Third Grade Skills* is a book that reinforces a variety of third grade basic skills.

- **Writing**
- **Grammar**
- **Literature**
- **Math**
- **Science**

This book was written with the wide range of student skills and ability levels of third grade students in mind. Both teachers and parents can benefit from the variety of pages provided in this book. Parents can use the book to provide an introduction to new material or to reinforce material already familiar to their children. Similarly, teachers can select pages that provide additional practice for concepts taught in the classroom. When tied to what is being covered in class, pages from this book make great homework reinforcement. The worksheets provided in this book are ideal for use at home as well as in the classroom. Research shows us that skill mastery comes with exposure and drill. To be internalized, concepts must be reviewed until they become second nature. Parents may certainly foster the classroom experience by exposing their children to the necessary skills whenever possible, and teachers will find that these pages perfectly complement their classroom needs. An answer key, beginning on page 163, provides teachers, parents, and children with a quick method of checking responses to completed work sheets.

Basic skills are utilized every day in untold ways. Make the practice of them part of your children's or students' routines. Such work done now will benefit them in countless ways throughout their lives.

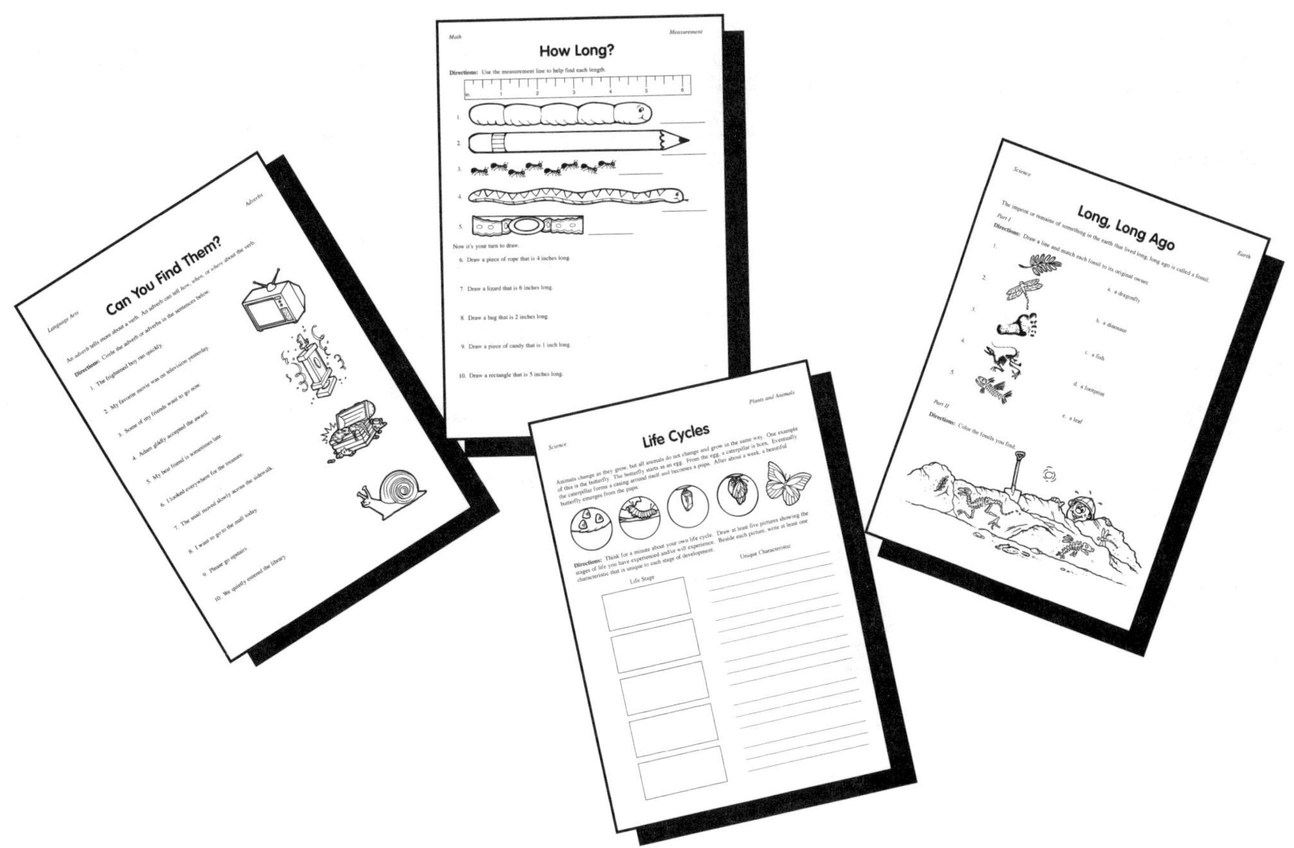

# A is for Apple

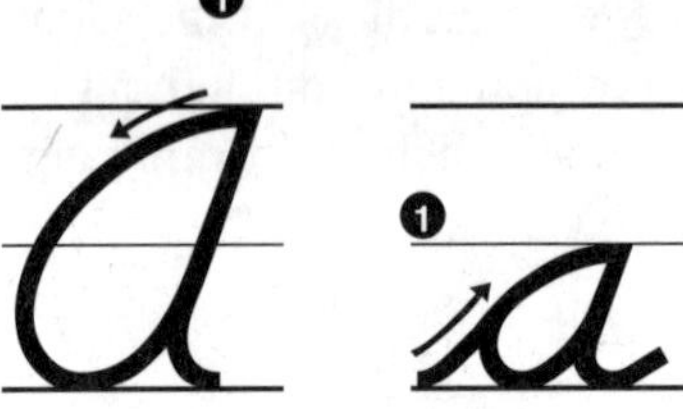

**Directions:** Trace each cursive letter and word. Write each letter four times. Practice writing each word.

A A

A A

a a

a a

Apple

Apple

apple

apple

# B is for Banana

B b

**Directions:** Trace each cursive letter and word. Write each letter four times. Practice writing each word.

B B

B B

b b

b b

Banana

Banana

banana

banana

# C is for Cat

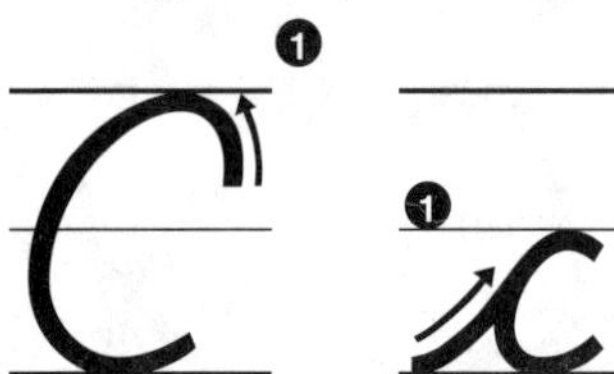

**Directions:** Trace each cursive letter and word. Write each letter four times. Practice writing each word.

C C

C C

c c

c c

Cat

Cat

cat

cat

 

# D is for Dog

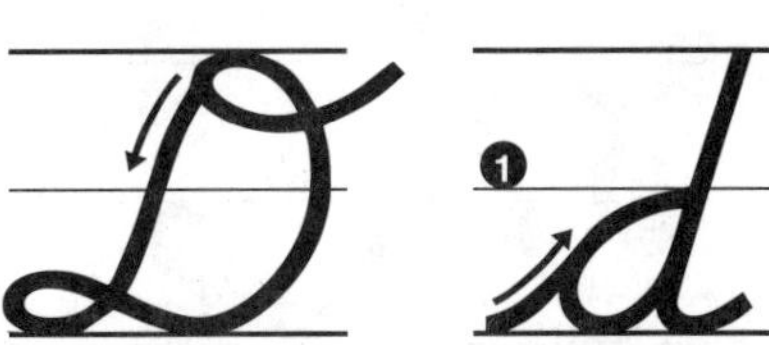

**Directions:** Trace each cursive letter and word. Write each letter four times. Practice writing each word.

D D

D D

d d

d d

Dog

Dog

dog

dog

# E is for Elk

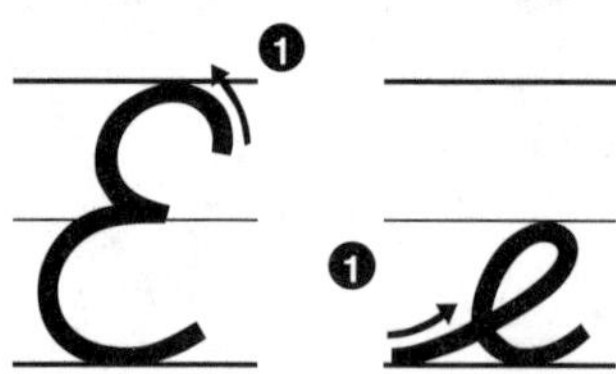

**Directions:** Trace each cursive letter and word. Write each letter four times. Practice writing each word.

E E

E E

e e

e e

Elk

Elk

elk

elk

# F is for Frog

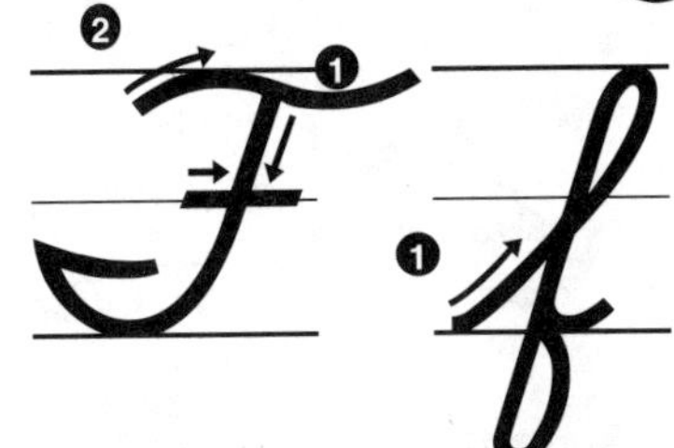

**Directions:** Trace each cursive letter and word. Write each letter four times. Practice writing each word.

F F

F F

f f

f f

Frog

Frog

frog

frog

# G is for Gerbil

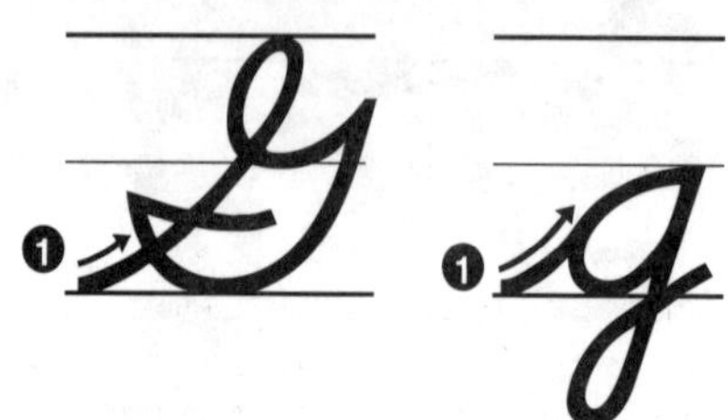

**Directions:** Trace each cursive letter and word. Write each letter four times. Practice writing each word.

G G

G G

g g

g g

Gerbil

Gerbil

gerbil

gerbil

# H is for Hat

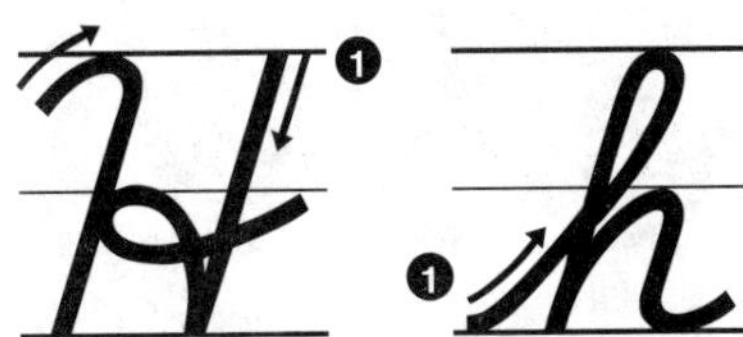

**Directions:** Trace each cursive letter and word. Write each letter four times. Practice writing each word.

H H

H H

h h

h h

Hat

Hat

hat

hat

# I is for Ice

**Directions:** Trace each cursive letter and word. Write each letter four times. Practice writing each word.

I I

I I

i i

i i

Ice

Ice

ice

ice

# J is for Jam

**Directions:** Trace each cursive letter and word. Write each letter four times. Practice writing each word.

J J

J J

j j

j j

Jam

Jam

jam

jam

# K is for Ketchup

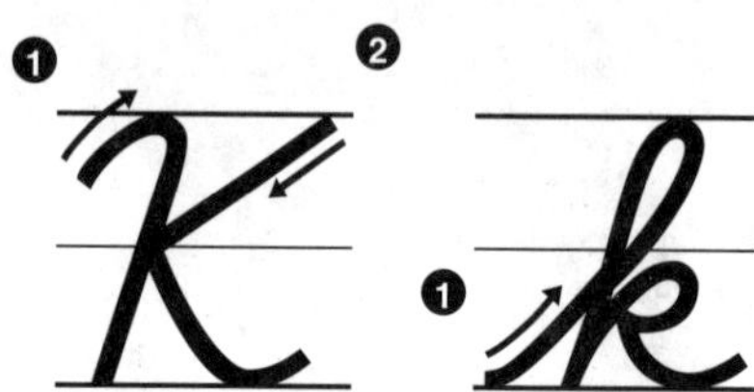

**Directions:** Trace each cursive letter and word. Write each letter four times. Practice writing each word.

K K

K K

k k

k k

Ketchup

Ketchup

ketchup

ketchup

 

# L is for Lemming

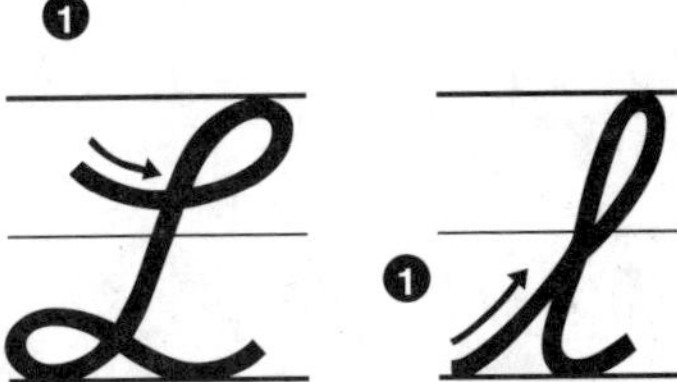

**Directions:** Trace each cursive letter and word. Write each letter four times. Practice writing each word.

L L

L L

l l

l l

Lemming

Lemming

lemming

lemming

# M is for Moose

M m

**Directions:** Trace each cursive letter and word. Write each letter four times. Practice writing each word.

M M

M M

m m

m m

Moose

Moose

moose

moose

# N is for Noodle

N n

**Directions:** Trace each cursive letter and word. Write each letter four times. Practice writing each word.

N N

N N

n n

n n

Noodle

Noodle

noodle

noodle

# O is for Octopus

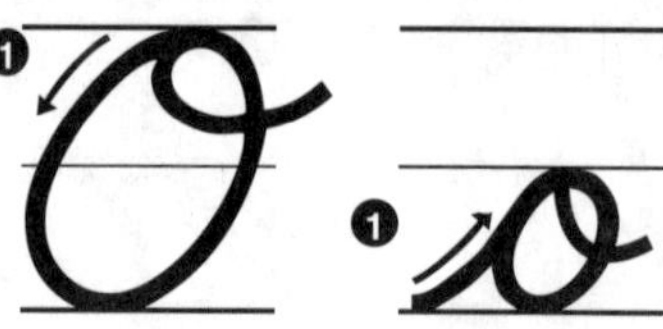

**Directions:** Trace each cursive letter and word. Write each letter four times. Practice writing each word.

O O

O O

o o

o o

Octopus

Octopus

octopus

octopus

# P is for Porcupine

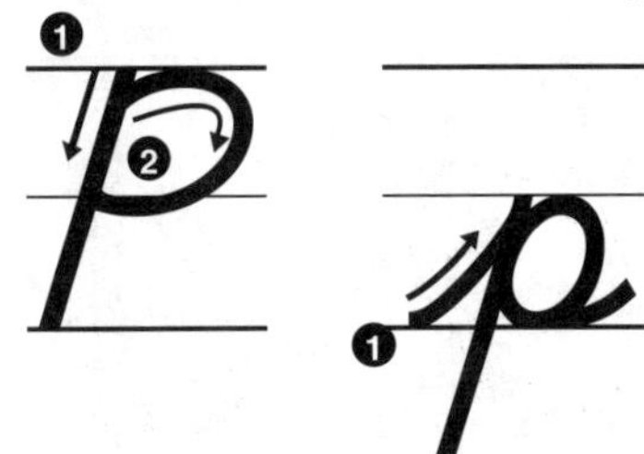

**Directions:** Trace each cursive letter and word. Write each letter four times. Practice writing each word.

P P

P P

p p

p p

Porcupine

Porcupine

porcupine

porcupine

# Q is for Quarter

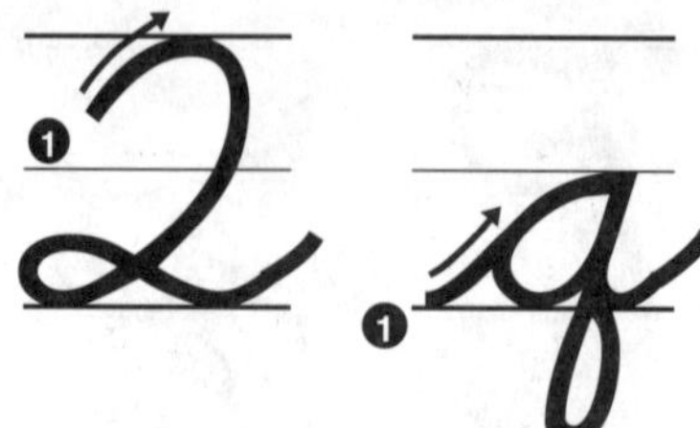

**Directions:** Trace each cursive letter and word. Write each letter four times. Practice writing each word.

Q Q

Q Q

q q

q q

Quarter

Quarter

quarter

quarter

# R is for Rabbit

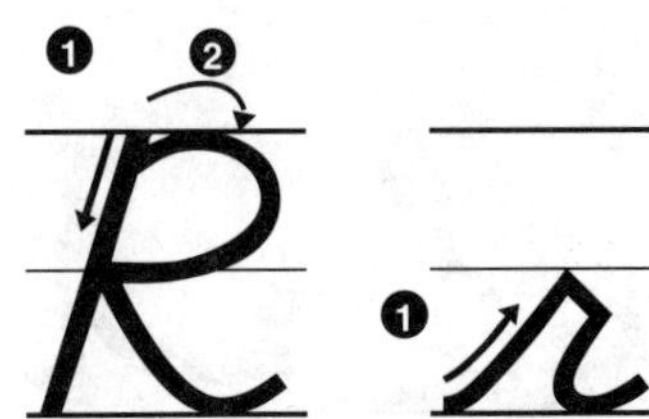

**Directions:** Trace each cursive letter and word. Write each letter four times. Practice writing each word.

R R

R R

r r

r r

Rabbit

Rabbit

rabbit

rabbit

# S is for Snowman

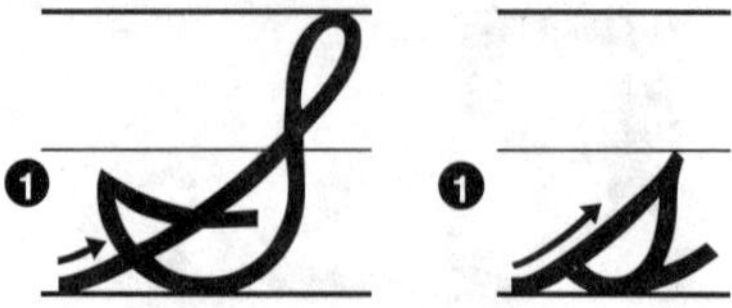

**Directions:** Trace each cursive letter and word. Write each letter four times. Practice writing each word.

S S

S S

s s

s s

Snowman

Snowman

snowman

snowman

 

# T is for Tree

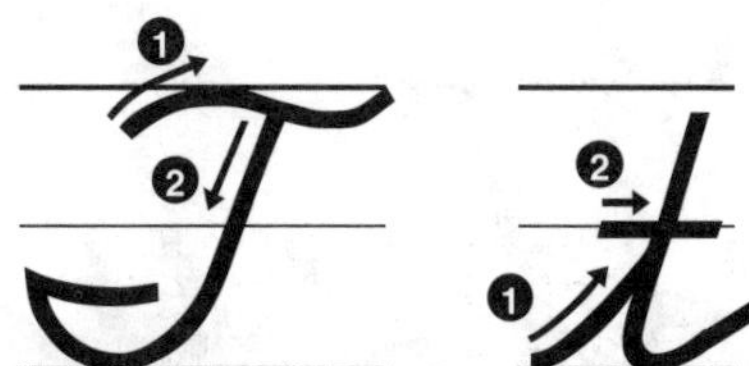

**Directions:** Trace each cursive letter and word. Write each letter four times. Practice writing each word.

T T

T T

t t

t t

Tree

Tree

tree

tree

# U is for Unicorn

U u

**Directions:** Trace each cursive letter and word. Write each letter four times. Practice writing each word.

U U

U U

u u

u u

Unicorn

Unicorn

unicorn

unicorn

# V is for Violin

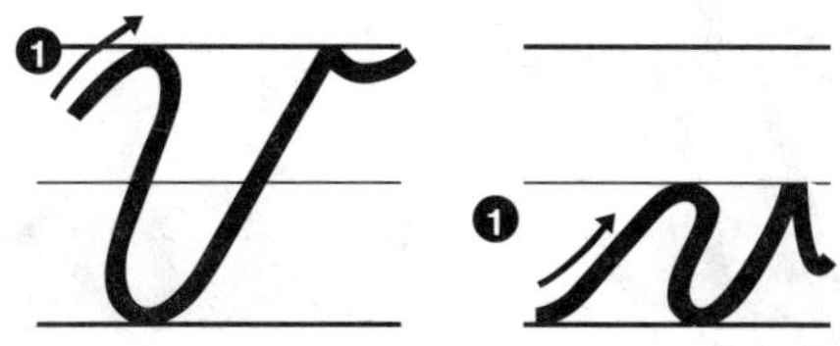

**Directions:** Trace each cursive letter and word. Write each letter four times. Practice writing each word.

V V

V V

v v

v v

Violin

Violin

violin

violin

# W is for Walrus

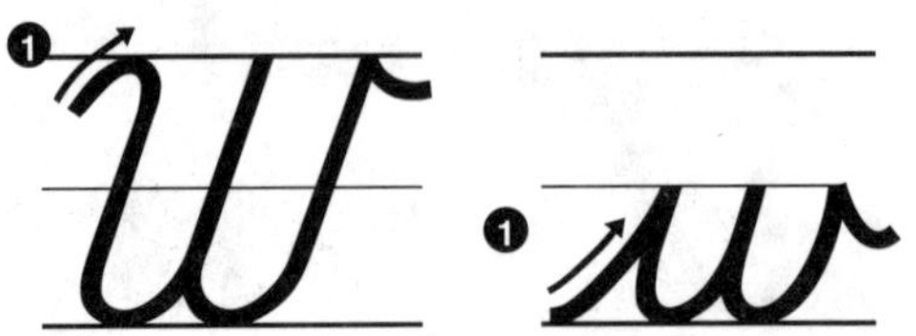

**Directions:** Trace each cursive letter and word. Write each letter four times. Practice writing each word.

W W

W W

w w

w w

Walrus

Walrus

walrus

walrus

# X is for X-ray

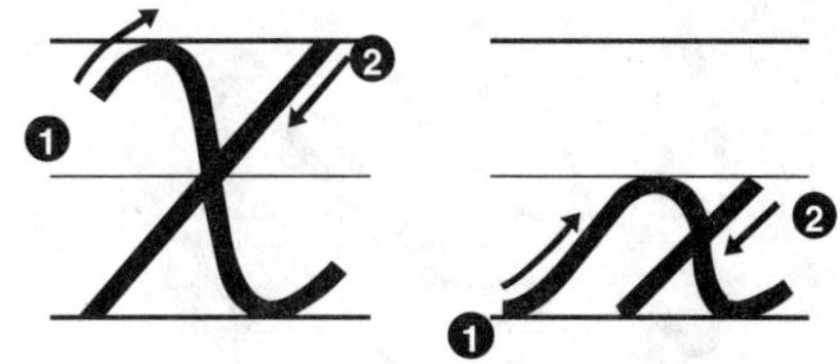

**Directions:** Trace each cursive letter and word. Write each letter four times. Practice writing each word.

X X

X X

x x

x x

X-ray

X-ray

x-ray

x-ray

# Y is for Yo-Yo

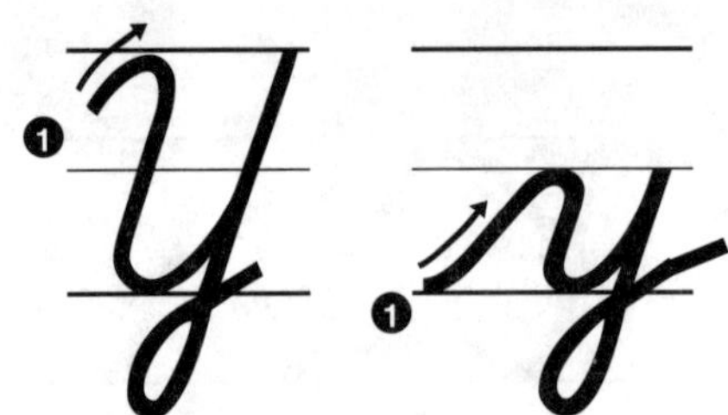

**Directions:** Trace each cursive letter and word. Write each letter four times. Practice writing each word.

Y Y

Y Y

y y

y y

Yo-yo

Yo-yo

yo-yo

yo-yo

# Z is for Zebra

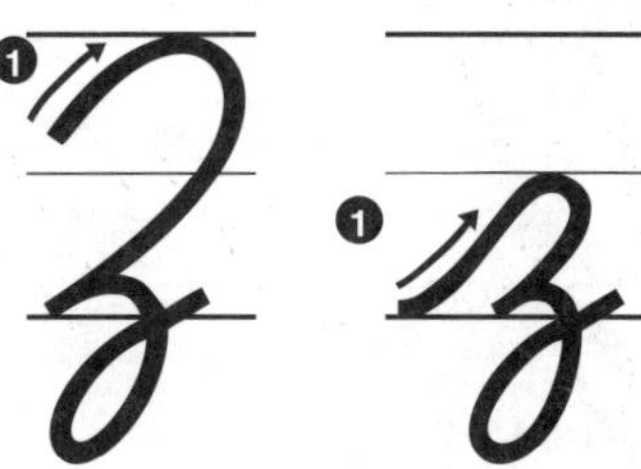

**Directions:** Trace each cursive letter and word. Write each letter four times. Practice writing each word.

Z Z
Z Z
z z
z z
Zebra
Zebra
zebra
zebra

# How Exciting!

An *exclamatory* sentence shows excitement or emotion.

*How great our field trip was!*

**Directions:** Read each question. Write an exclamatory sentence to answer each question.

**Example:** Can you believe you had a surprise party?

*Gosh, the party was a total surprise to me!*

1. Did you have a good birthday? ______________________________

______________________________

2. What was your favorite present? ______________________________

______________________________

3. Were the clowns funny? ______________________________

______________________________

4. How fun was your party? ______________________________

______________________________

5. Did everyone have a good time at the party? ______________________________

______________________________

6. How much cake and ice cream did you eat? ______________________________

______________________________

 

# Simon Says

In the game Simon Says everyone has to obey Simon's commands. An *imperative* or *command* sentence is a lot like Simon. This type of sentence tells or asks someone to do something.

**Examples**: Please, sit down.

Sit down now.

**Directions:** Read each sentence. If the sentence is a command, write the letter C on the line.

1. Go to the office. _________
2. How wonderful you look! _________
3. Sit next to me. _________
4. Answer the phone. _________
5. Do you know my name? _________
6. Give me more dessert. _________
7. Chocolate pie is delicious. _________
8. Get ready to go. _________
9. I love you. _________
10. Answer the next question. _________

# Being Agreeable

A *pronoun* is a word that takes the place of a noun. A pronoun must match in number and gender the noun that it replaces.

**Examples:** Karen is my friend.

She is very nice.

You wouldn't write "He is nice" because Karen is a girl, not a boy.

*Part I*

**Directions:** Circle the correct pronoun in each sentence.

1. Jake lost (his, her) notebook.
2. The family is going on vacation because (they, it) want to visit Vancouver.
3. My mother bought a diamond ring and she put it in (his, her) safe.
4. The children went to the movies, and (it, they) bought a lot of popcorn to eat.
5. Sally gave (her, its) parents a gift for their anniversary.

*Part II*

**Directions:** Circle the words that are pronouns.

| | | |
|---|---|---|
| candy | he | dog |
| she | week | chair |
| it | they | you |
| me | little | I |
| to | us | we |

 

# Match Them Up

A *pronoun* is a word that takes the place of a noun.

**Directions:** Match each pronoun piece to the correct noun piece by coloring both pieces the same color.

# Name That Picture

A *noun* that is singular names one person, place, or thing.

**Directions:** Look at each picture. On the lines provided, write the singular noun that names each picture.

**1.**

______________________

**2.**

______________________

**3.**

______________________

**4.**

______________________

**5.**

______________________

**6.**

______________________

**7.**

______________________

**8.**

______________________

**9.**

______________________

**10.**

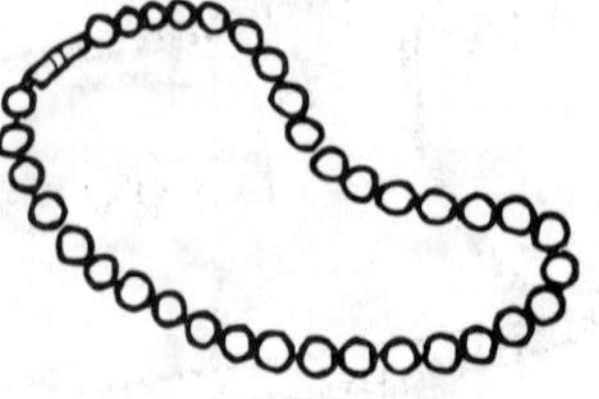

______________________

# Just Add an SSSSS

To make a noun plural, you usually add the letter *S*.

**Directions:** Change each noun to a plural noun by adding the letter *S*. Write the new word on the line provided.

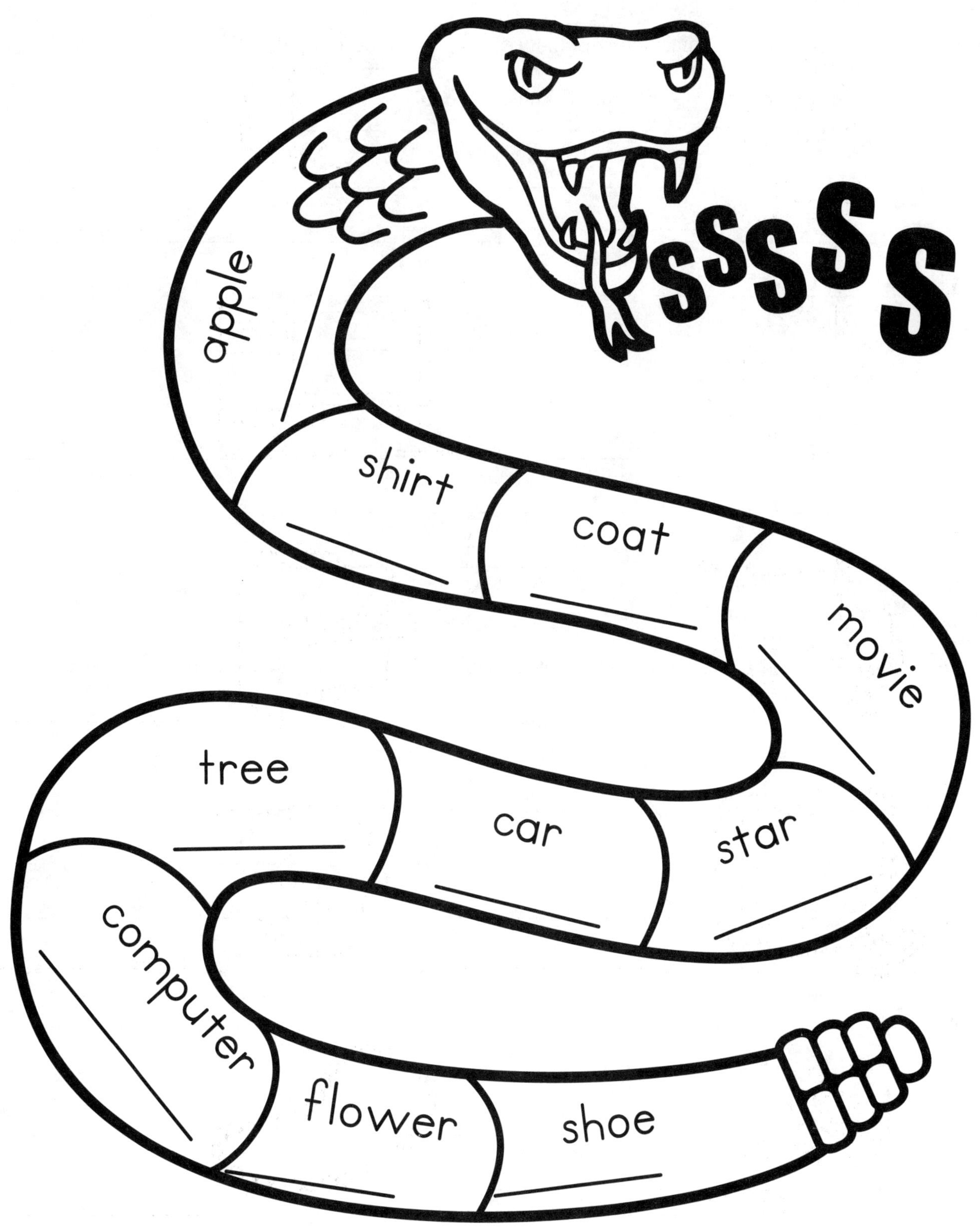

# Singular or Plural?

A *singular noun* names one person, place, or thing.

A *plural noun* names more than one person, place, or thing.

*Part I*

**Directions:** Look at the singular nouns in the word bank. Write a sentence using each of these nouns.

| cat | house | book | ball |
|---|---|---|---|

1. ______________________________

______________________________

2. ______________________________

______________________________

3. ______________________________

______________________________

4. ______________________________

______________________________

*Part II*

**Directions:** Look at the plural nouns in the word bank. Write a sentence using each of these nouns.

| kids | teams | pizzas | students |
|---|---|---|---|

1. ______________________________

______________________________

2. ______________________________

______________________________

3. ______________________________

______________________________

4. ______________________________

______________________________

# Something Different

Most nouns become plural by adding the letter *s* or *es*. However, some nouns need different endings.

| | |
|---|---|
| cherry | cherries |
| child | children |
| mouse | mice |

**Directions:** Write the plural form of each noun.

1. goose ______________________
2. story ______________________
3. man ______________________
4. ox ______________________
5. leaf ______________________
6. berry ______________________
7. lady ______________________
8. deer ______________________
9. penny ______________________
10. woman ______________________

# Proper and Common

*A proper noun* is always capitalized. *A common noun* is not capitalized. *A proper noun* names a specific person, place, or thing. A *common noun* is not specific.

| **Proper** | **Common** |
|---|---|
| Jeffrey | boy |
| Ontario | city |

**Directions:** Read each sentence. Draw a circle around any proper nouns. Place an X on any common nouns.

1. Jennifer always gets pizza for supper on Fridays.

2. My friend is a nice person.
3. Can you and Joe bake the cake?
4. Mom and Dad are going to the game.
5. Chloe and Kayla Beth are sisters.

6. The bus took the students to school.
7. Ella gave the teacher an apple.

8. Gage gave the teacher a pencil.
9. Sally saw a huge snake in the tree.
10. The day was Tuesday.

 

# An Interesting Subject

The *subject* of a sentence is who or what it's all about. A noun can be the subject of a sentence.

**Directions:** Each sentence is missing its subject. Supply a subject by writing a noun on each line.

1. My ________________ is broken so I can't use it.

2. My favorite ________________ is chocolate pie.

3. Her birthday ________________ is next Saturday.

4. The ugly ________________ scared me.

5. Walruses, whales, and ________________ are sea mammals.

6. ________________ is great fun.

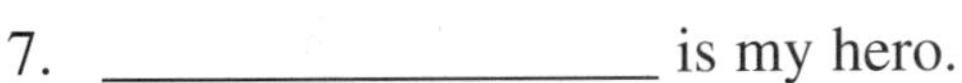

7. ________________ is my hero.

8. A large ________________ was in my mom's car.

# Simple Subjects and Simple Predicates

The *simple subject* of a sentence is who or what it's all about. The simple subject is usually a noun. The *simple predicate* of a sentence is what the subject is doing, or it is a word that links the subject to something else.

*Dee walks home from school.*

The simple subject is *Dee*. The simple predicate is *walks*.

*Dee is finally home.*

The simple subject is *Dee*. The simple predicate is the word *is*.

**Directions:** Look at each column. Choose a subject and a predicate. Then use the words in a sentence of your own. You need to write five sentences. If needed, you can add the letters *ed* or *ing* to each predicate.

| **Subjects** | **Predicates** |
|---|---|
| cat | swims |
| tree | walks |
| boy | ran |
| Karen | talks |
| car | is |
| school | are |
| teacher | jumps |
| Ken | yells |

1. ______________________________

   ______________________________

2. ______________________________

   ______________________________

3. ______________________________

   ______________________________

4. ______________________________

   ______________________________

5. ______________________________

   ______________________________

 

# Action!

*Action verbs* are what you do. *Play*, *skip*, and *hop* are all examples of action verbs.

**Directions:** Find your way from start to finish by coloring only the blocks that have words which can be action verbs.

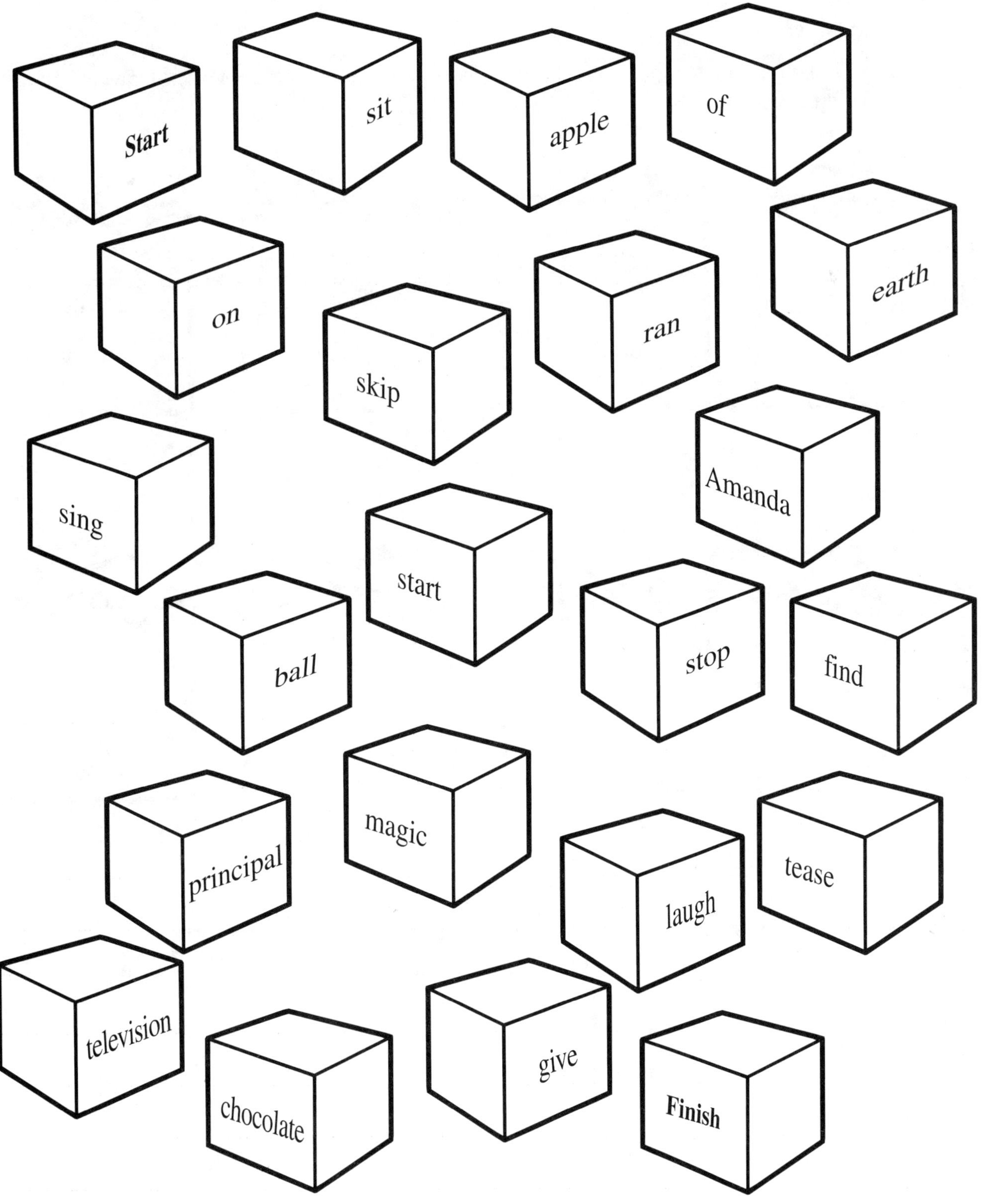

# Past or Present

Some verbs tell about things that are happening right now. These are *present-tense* verbs.

*I cry at sad movies.*

Some verbs tell about things that have happened in the past. These are *past-tense* verbs.

*I cried at the sad movie.*

**Directions:** Each present contains two verbs. Circle the verb that is present tense. Draw a square around the verb that is past tense.

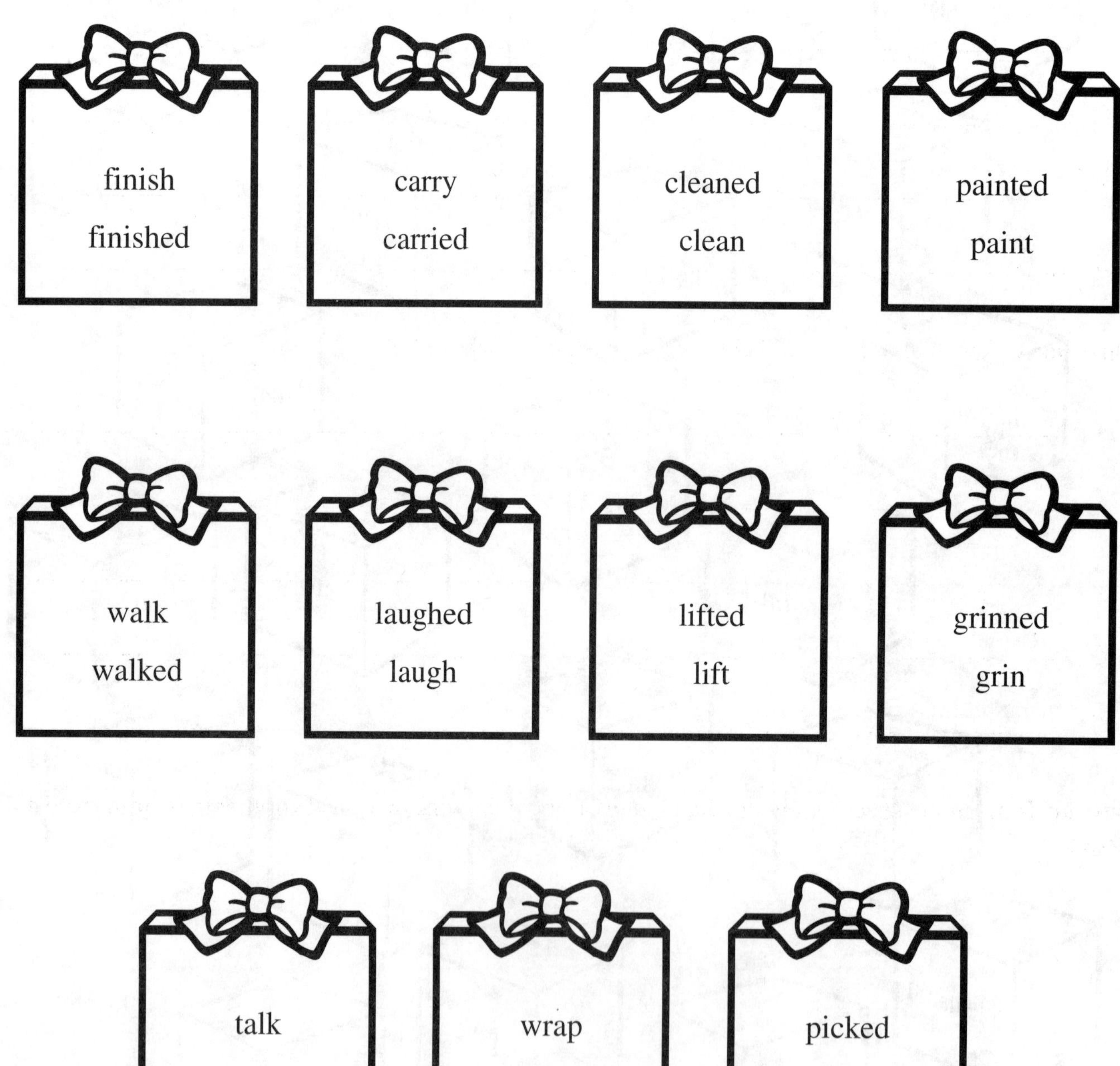


 

# What Did You Do? When Did You Do It?

Verbs can change tenses. Some verbs are *present tense*, which means the action is happening now, and some are *past tense*, which means the action has happened already.

**Directions:** List five things you did yesterday. Be sure to use past tense verbs.

1. ______________________________

2. ______________________________

3. ______________________________

4. ______________________________

5. ______________________________

**Directions:** List five things you like to do. Use present tense verbs.

1. ______________________________

2. ______________________________

3. ______________________________

4. ______________________________

5. ______________________________

**Just for fun:** In the space below draw a picture of you doing one of your favorite things from the list above.

# Describe It

An *adjective* is a word that describes a noun.

**Directions:** List two adjectives that can describe each noun.

**Example:** apple red and shiny

1. boy ____________ and ____________
2. girl ____________ and ____________
3. school ____________ and ____________
4. dog ____________ and ____________
5. home ____________ and ____________
6. summer ____________ and ____________
7. cars ____________ and ____________
8. sports ____________ and ____________
9. pizza ____________ and ____________
10. flowers ____________ and ____________

 

# More with Adjectives

*Adjectives* describe nouns. They tell *how many, which one,* or *what kind* of noun it is.

Many friends *how many*

Those friends *which ones*

Great friends *what kind*

**Directions:** Read each sentence. Color each underlined adjective according to the directions below.

If the adjective tells *how many*, color the word *yellow*.

If the adjective tells *which one*, color the word *blue*.

If the adjective tells *what kind*, color the word *orange*.

1. These grapes are delicious!
2. I like red grapes the best.
3. My favorite grocery store sells the best grapes.
4. Some people only like green grapes.
5. No matter the kind of grapes you like, fresh fruit is always the best.
6. A few grapes are always good to eat each and every day.
7. Whatever you do, don't eat any shriveled grapes!
8. Several friends of mine think I'm crazy to like grapes so much.
9. Maybe they've just never had enough of the delicious fruit.
10. I know I can never get enough of those wonderful grapes.

# Telling More about Verbs

*Adverbs* tell us more about verbs. Adverbs tell *where*, *when*, or *how* about verbs.

| | |
|---|---|
| We ran quickly. | *how* |
| Yesterday we ran. | *when* |
| We ran upstairs. | *where* |

*Part I*

**Directions:** Look at each question. Use adverbs from the word bank below to describe each event.

| | | | | |
|---|---|---|---|---|
| soon | tomorrow | today | early | late |
| inside | outside | slowly | quickly | last |
| first | next | easily | carefully | now |

1. Do you get up ____________ or ____________ on the weekends?
2. Would you rather be ____________ or ____________ on a cold day?
3. If you were running in a race, would you rather finish ____________ or ____________ ?
4. The day after today is ____________ .
5. If you are carrying something breakable, you should carry it ____________ .

*Part II*

**Directions:** Choose five adverbs from the list above and use them in sentences of your own.

6. ______________________________________________________________

______________________________________________________________

7. ______________________________________________________________

______________________________________________________________

8. ______________________________________________________________

______________________________________________________________

9. ______________________________________________________________

______________________________________________________________

10. ______________________________________________________________

______________________________________________________________

# Can You Find Them?

An *adverb* tells more about a verb. An adverb can tell *how, when,* or *where* about the verb.

**Directions:** Circle the adverb or adverbs in the sentences below.

1. The frightened boy ran quickly.

2. My favorite movie was on television yesterday.

3. Some of my friends want to go now.

4. Adam gladly accepted the award.

5. My best friend is sometimes late.

6. I looked everywhere for the treasure.

7. The snail moved slowly across the sidewalk.

8. I want to go to the mall today.

9. Please go upstairs.

10. We quietly entered the library.

# Know When to Capitalize

Some nouns need to be capitalized. These nouns are called *proper nouns*. They name a specific person, place, or thing.

The *girl* did her homework.

*Casey* did her homework.

*Casey* names a specific girl and so needs to be capitalized.

**Directions:** Answer each question. Be sure to capitalize any proper nouns that you use.

1. What is your favorite day of the week?________________________________________

2. What is your favorite month? ________________________________________

3. In what month were you born? ________________________________________

4. What is your last name? ________________________________________

5. What is your favorite holiday? ________________________________________

6. What is the name of your favorite restaurant? ______________________________

7. What is your favorite sports team? ________________________________________

8. In what city do you live?________________________________________

9. In what country do you live?________________________________________

10. What is the name of your favorite movie? ______________________________

 

# Say It with Capitals

When using quotation marks, capitalize the first letter of the word after the first quotation mark.

**Example:** Kristen said, “My sister Allison is my best friend.”

**Directions:** Read each quote. Answer with a quote of your own. Be sure to use correct capitalization.

1. Derek said, “Do you want to play with me?”

   Shea replied, “ ________________________________________ .”

2. He asked, “How old are you?”

   She answered, “ ________________________________________ .”

3. “Can I help you?” he asked.

   “ ________________________________________ ,” she responded.

4. Tessa said, “You are a nice brother, Simon.”

   Simon replied, “ ________________________________________ .”

5. Mark asked, “Could you please keep your room neater?”

   Amanda answered, “ ________________________________________ .”

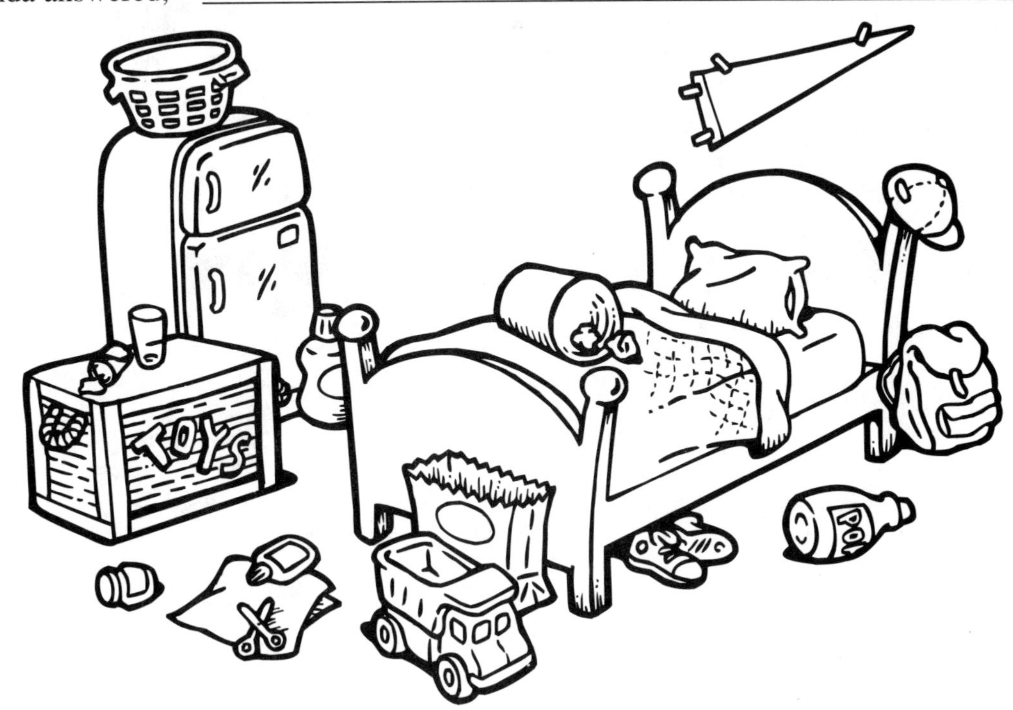

# More Than a Dot

A *period* is much more than just a dot. Use a period in initials, abbreviations, and with certain titles before names.

| | |
|---|---|
| *Carla Jean Smith* | *C. J. Smith* |
| *Drive* | *Dr.* |
| *Mister Jones* | *Mr. Jones* |

**Directions:** Look at the spots on the dog below. Each one contains a punctuation mistake. Add periods as needed to correct the problems.

# It's All in the End

End a statement or a command with a *period*.

**Example:** Your hair looks icky.

Go wash your hair.

**Directions:** Finish each statement or command and add the correct ending punctuation.

1. I really like ______________________________
2. Move that ______________________________
3. Get me a ______________________________
4. Chris is a ______________________________
5. Go to the ______________________________
6. We ate ______________________________
7. I hate when ______________________________
8. Take a ______________________________
9. Look at ______________________________
10. Give me ______________________________

# Two into One

An *apostrophe* shows where letters are missing. When two words are made into a new word, that new word is called a *contraction*.

By using an apostrophe, *do not* becomes *don't*. The apostrophe takes the place of the *o* in *not*.

**Directions:** Draw a line and match each set of words to the correct contraction.

| | |
|---|---|
| 1. does not | a. weren't |
| 2. will not | b. aren't |
| 3. has not | c. hadn't |
| 4. was not | d. doesn't |
| 5. is not | e. Jack's |
| 6. did not | f. hasn't |
| 7. had not | g. wasn't |
| 8. were not | h. isn't |
| 9. are not | i. didn't |
| 10. Jack is | j. won't |

 

# What Was It?

An *apostrophe* shows where letters are missing. When two words are made into a new word, that new word is called a *contraction.*

*Is not* becomes *isn't*. The letter that is missing is the letter *o*, which has been replaced by an apostrophe.

**Directions:** Read each sentence. Circle the contraction in each sentence. Then, on the line provided, write the two words that make up the contraction.

1. I don't really like him. ______________________
2. She isn't my friend. ______________________
3. Olivia can't come to the party. ______________________
4. We aren't the only ones going. ______________________
5. He doesn't act like a teacher. ______________________
6. I haven't found my money yet. ______________________
7. Michele's going to the movies. ______________________
8. Natalie won't stop crying. ______________________
9. He's my father's best friend. ______________________
10. Kimberly and Courtney didn't leave. ______________________

# Playing Genie

An apostrophe can be used with a noun to show possession or ownership. If Kara owns a cat then the apostrophe can help show that it is *Kara's* cat.

**Directions:** Imagine you are a genie in a bottle and instead of giving out just the standard three wishes, you can grant 10 wishes to anyone you want. Make the following kids' wishes come true by writing and using an apostrophe to give them what they want.

**Example:** Joe wants a skateboard. *Joe's skateboard*

1. Emily wants some candy. ____________________
2. Chien wants a DVD. ____________________
3. Tyrese wants a new backpack. ____________________
4. Rafael wants a camera. ____________________
5. Keysha wants a necklace. ____________________
6. Elissa wants a game. ____________________
7. Sharon wants a puzzle. ____________________
8. Samuel wants some shoes. ____________________
9. Aina wants a book. ____________________
10. Brody wants a bike. ____________________

# Talk to Me

*Quotation marks* are used to show that someone is speaking. They come at the beginning and the end of a person's words.

**Example:** Riley asked, "Do you know the words to this song?"

Quotation marks are not around *Riley asked* because Riley didn't say those words.

**Directions:** Pretend you have just given your teacher an apple, but when she bit into the delicious treat, she bit into a juicy worm!

What would you say? What would your teacher say to you?

On the lines provided write a short conversation between you and your teacher. Remember to use quotation marks around what was said.

Also, be sure to start on a new line each time you change speakers. This makes your conversation easier to read.

# Quotation Marks Mark the Spot

*Quotation marks* go around a person's exact words. If there is a comma before the quotation, it goes outside the quotation marks. Punctuation at the end of a quotation goes inside the quotation marks.

**Example:** He said, "I don't want to go."

"But you must be there," she replied.

**Directions:** Read each quote and add quotation marks wherever they are needed.

1. I can't wait for summer vacation, Ted said.
2. I can't wait either, Addison agreed.
3. Where are you going on vacation? Ted asked.
4. We're going to Hawaii, Addison said.
5. That sounds very nice, Ted replied.
6. Where are you going? Addison asked.
7. Ted replied, Well, it's not exactly Hawaii, but there is water there.
8. Well, where is it? Addison asked again.
9. I'm going to spend my vacation working at my Uncle Bob's carwash, Ted finally told her.
10. I guess you're right. There will be plenty of water, Addison said with a smile.

# Not Quite Human

*Personification* is when a nonliving object is given human characteristics. How can you remember this? Notice the root word of personification is *person*. If a nonliving object is given human characteristics then the writer has used personification.

**Example:** The sand on the beach ran its grainy fingers along our bare feet.

**Directions:** Circle the sentences that show examples of personification.

1. I love spaghetti and meatballs.
2. The burnt spaghetti stared at me sadly from my plate.
3. The delicious smell of spaghetti called to me from the kitchen.
4. I don't know which I love more, spaghetti or lasagna.
5. The noodles and red sauce begged for me to eat them.
6. I swallowed them quickly and then hurried to get more.
7. I love spaghetti and my spaghetti loves me.
8. The delicious noodles danced their way to my tummy.
9. If the spaghetti was this good, I knew the dessert would be even better.
10. I heard the chef was serving chocolate-covered spaghetti noodles.

# Watch That Twisting Tongue!

*Alliteration* is the repetition of a sound. Tongue-twisters are examples of alliteration.

**Example:** She sells seashells down by the seashore.

Notice the repetition of the *S* sound.

**Directions:** Use alliteration to write your own tongue-twisters.

1. Write a tongue-twister using the sound of the letter *T*.

___________________________________________

___________________________________________

___________________________________________

2. Write a tongue-twister using the sound of the letter *S*.

___________________________________________

___________________________________________

___________________________________________

3. Write a tongue-twister using the sound of the letter *Z*.

___________________________________________

___________________________________________

___________________________________________

4. Write a tongue-twister using the sound of the letter *R*.

___________________________________________

___________________________________________

___________________________________________

**Just for fun:** In the space below draw an illustration for one of your tongue-twisters.

 

# Splat! Bam! Boom!

*Onomatopoeia* is when a word is used to represent a sound. A bee doesn't really go "buzz," but we use the word *buzz* to represent the sound a bee makes.

**Directions:** Beside each word write an example of onomatopoeia for the sound each thing makes.

1. A dog wanting attention ____________________
2. A cat wanting some milk ____________________
3. A door shutting hard ____________________
4. A door that needs some oil ____________________
5. A girl eating a piece of ice ____________________
6. A balloon being stuck with a nail ____________________
7. A baby crying ____________________
8. A librarian warning you to be quiet ____________________
9. A crowd cheering for a team ____________________
10. A baby bird wanting a snack ____________________

# This is Like That

A *simile* is a comparison that uses the words *like* or *as* to make the comparison.

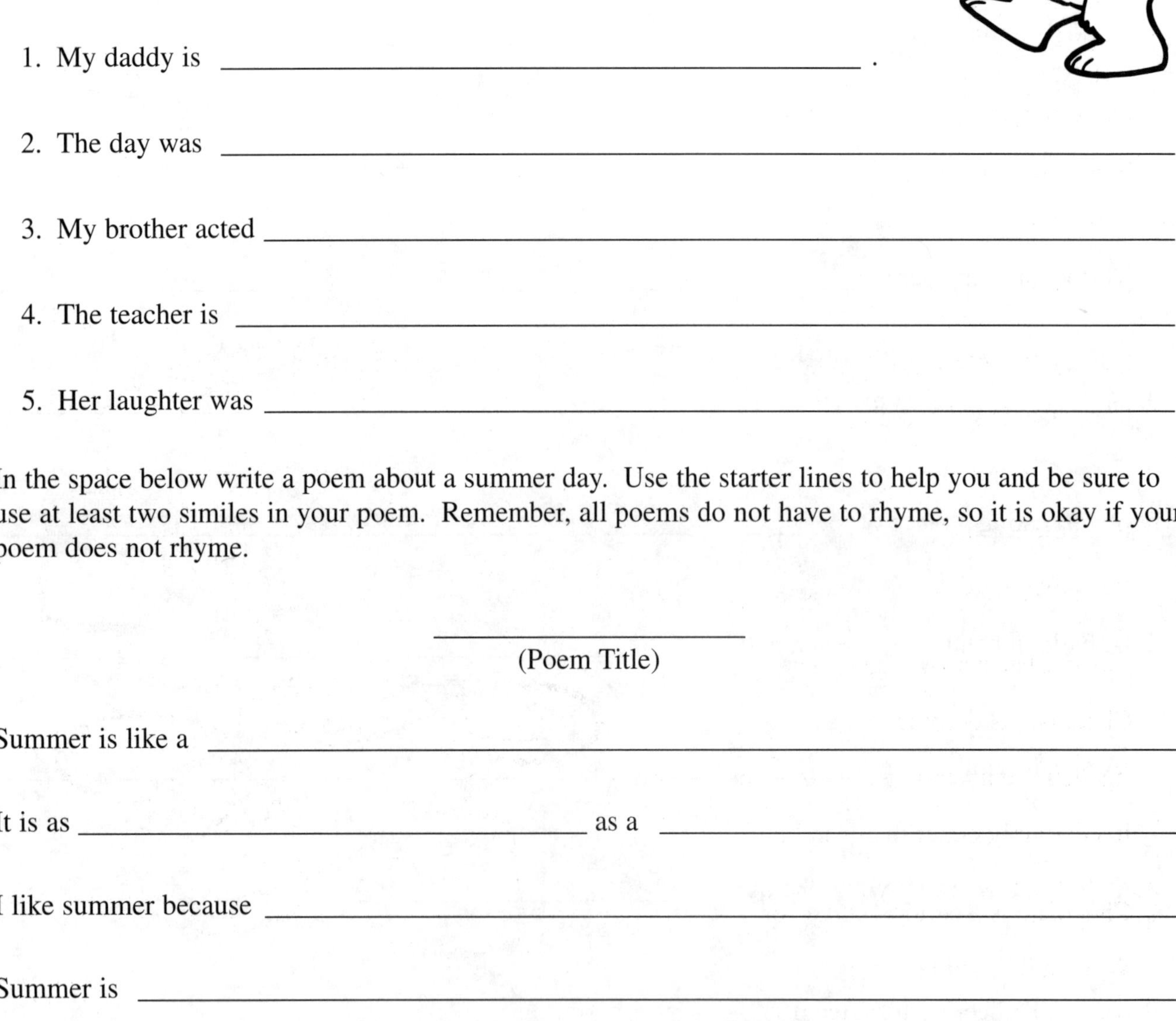

**Example:** My blanket is like a warm, fuzzy bear.

My blanket is as warm as a soft, fuzzy bear.

The blanket is being compared to a warm, fuzzy bear.

**Directions:** Complete each sentence starter with a simile.

1. My daddy is ______________________________ .
2. The day was ______________________________ .
3. My brother acted ______________________________ .
4. The teacher is ______________________________ .
5. Her laughter was ______________________________ .

In the space below write a poem about a summer day. Use the starter lines to help you and be sure to use at least two similes in your poem. Remember, all poems do not have to rhyme, so it is okay if your poem does not rhyme.

______________________

(Poem Title)

Summer is like a ______________________________

It is as ____________________ as a ____________________

I like summer because ______________________________

Summer is ______________________________

 

# It Is What It Is

A *metaphor* is a comparison that does not use *like* or *as*.

**Example:** That boy is a pig.

Is the boy really a pig? Of course not! A metaphor is simply a comparison. Maybe the boy is very messy or maybe he eats a lot.

**Directions:** Read the poem below. Circle all metaphors in the poem.

**Chocolate**

Of all the things I love the most,
Some are not that strange.
I love my mother and my father
And even my sister, Lorraine.

But my favorite thing is chocolate.
Chocolate is a dream.
It melts in my mouth.
It is gold for the tongue.
It is always a delicious thing.

I love it because it's easy to get.
Chocolate is definitely heaven.
It's better than caramel or strawberry swirl,
It's certainly better than vanilla.

Chocolate is a cartoon character,
With smiles and laughs for all.
When I eat chocolate, I am so happy;
I feel like I'm ten feet tall!

# Bigger and Better

A *hyperbole* is an extreme exaggeration. For example, your big brother might be tall, but if you say that he's so tall he could reach the top of the Empire State Building, then that's an extreme exaggeration.

*Part I*

**Directions:** Complete each sentence with a hyperbole of your own.

**Example:** My cousin is so smart that teachers ask her if the answers are correct or not.

1. My sister is so little ______________________________.
2. My teacher is so mean ______________________________.
3. My school is so big ______________________________.
4. My friends are so nice ______________________________.

*Part II*

**Directions:** Read each statement. If the statement is a hyperbole, write the letter H on the line provided. If it is not a hyperbole, write an X on the line.

______ 5. Her appetite is so big she can eat every bit of food in the grocery store.

______ 6. She is the nicest person I know.

______ 7. This weather is so cold it would make a penguin wear a coat.

______ 8. My head really, really hurts.

# Where Is It?

The *setting* of a story includes all the places where the story happens or takes place. For example, in the story of "The Three Little Pigs," the setting includes all three homes where the pigs live. The straw house, the stick house, and the brick house are all part of the setting.

**Directions:** Look at each picture. On the line provided, describe each setting.

**Example:**  The setting is a tropical and nearly deserted island.

1.  ______________________________

2.  ______________________________

3.  ______________________________

4.  ______________________________

5.  ______________________________

6.  ______________________________

# And the Answer Is...

When you *draw a conclusion* you tell what you think the outcome is going to be. For example, if your class has a field trip to the zoo planned but on the day of the field trip there is a storm, you can probably conclude that the field trip will be canceled.

**Directions:** Read each situation and then write what you think the conclusion will be.

1. A little boy brings home a report card with straight As.

______________________________________________

______________________________________________

______________________________________________

2. A woman sees a dog digging up flowers in her front yard.

______________________________________________

______________________________________________

______________________________________________

3. A little girl leaves her ice-cream cone outside in the hot sun.

______________________________________________

______________________________________________

______________________________________________

4. A truck is going down a road. Just ahead there are nails scattered on the road.

______________________________________________

______________________________________________

______________________________________________

5. A mother bird is sitting on her nest. One of her eggs starts to crack.

______________________________________________

______________________________________________

______________________________________________

 

# One Thing Leads to Another

Every *effect* has a *cause*. If you forget to bring your coat to school and it snows while you are at school, you will be cold when it's time to go home.

**Example:** *Effect:* You are cold.

*Cause:* You forgot your coat.

**Directions:** Match each cause to the correct effect.

1. You have a toothache.
2. You don't do your homework.
3. You forget to water your plants.
4. You have a birthday party.
5. You work outside in the hot sun.

A. You make a bad grade.
B. They do not grow.
C. You get a lot of presents.
D. You get a sunburn.
E. You go to the dentist.

Now write a cause and effect for each space below.

6. ______________________________

______________________________

______________________________

7. ______________________________

______________________________

______________________________

8. ______________________________

______________________________

______________________________

9. ______________________________

______________________________

______________________________

10. ______________________________

______________________________

______________________________

# How Would You Behave?

If you are reading a story, you may use *inference* to help you predict how a character will or will not behave. Inference is a guess you make based on what you know.

For example, imagine a very strict teacher who always expects her class to behave. If she has to leave the room for a minute, then comes back to the classroom and the students are throwing paper airplanes and running around the room, how do you think she will react?

If you guessed that she would not be pleased, then you are using inference.

**Directions:** Read each situation and infer the reaction. Write your answer on the lines provided.

1. A young boy has a piggy bank filled with change. His little sister sneaks in his room and accidentally breaks his bank. The young boy walks into his room and sees change all over the place and his sister looking guilty.

   How do you think he might react? ______________________________

   ______________________________

2. A brother and sister get out of bed on a school day and rush to the window. It is snowing outside! They both received sleds for their birthdays and have been wishing for a snow day to try out their new gifts. Their mother comes into the room and tells them school has been canceled.

   How do you think they might react? ______________________________

   ______________________________

   ______________________________

   ______________________________

3. An ice-cream truck is coming down the street. A little girl has money and wants to buy some ice cream. On her way to the truck, she sees a sign that says "Puppy for Sale". The puppy costs the same amount of money that the little girl has in her hand. She knows her mother and daddy don't want her to have a puppy, but she's always wanted one.

   What do you think she might do? ______________________________

   ______________________________

   ______________________________

   ______________________________

   ______________________________

# Addition Magician

**Directions:** Add to find the sum.

1. 

2. 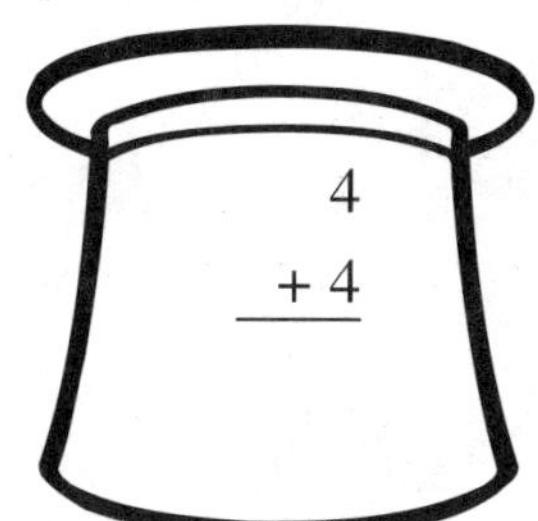


3. 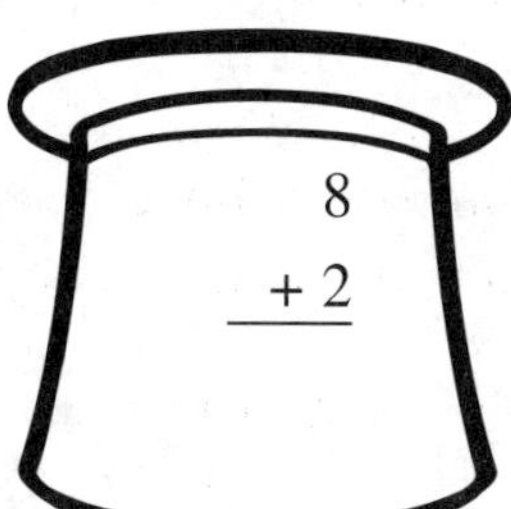


4. 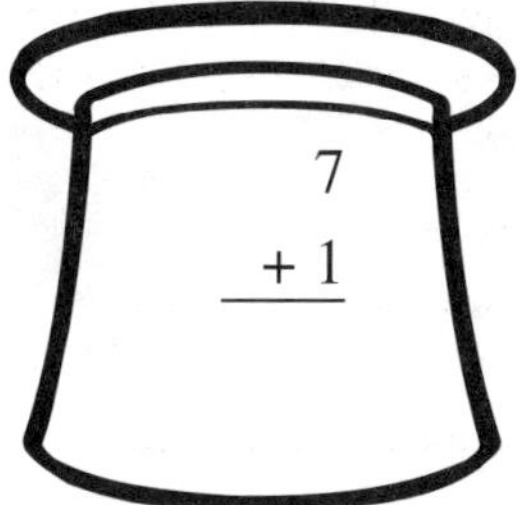


5. 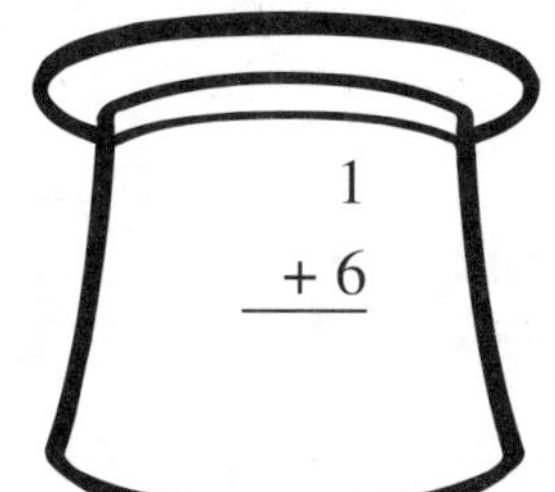


6. 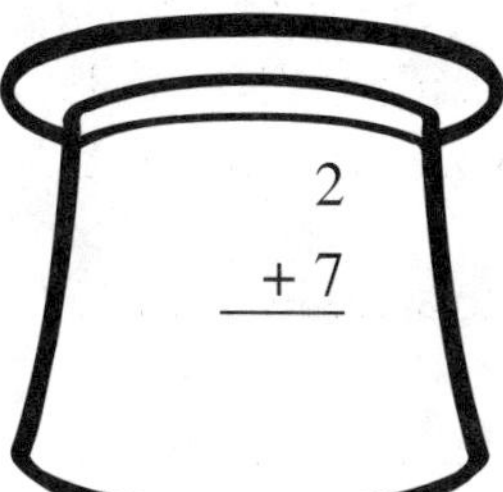


7. 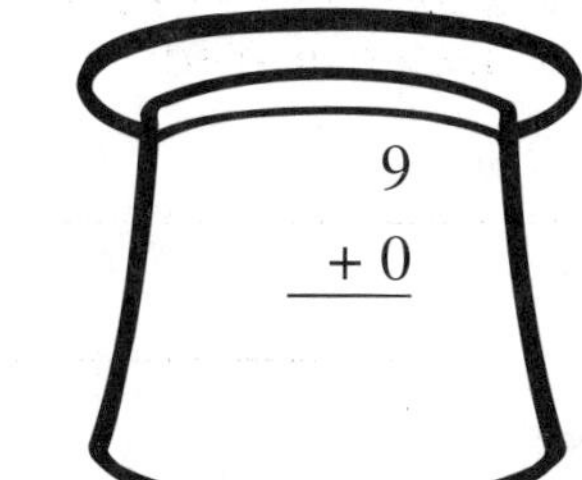


8. 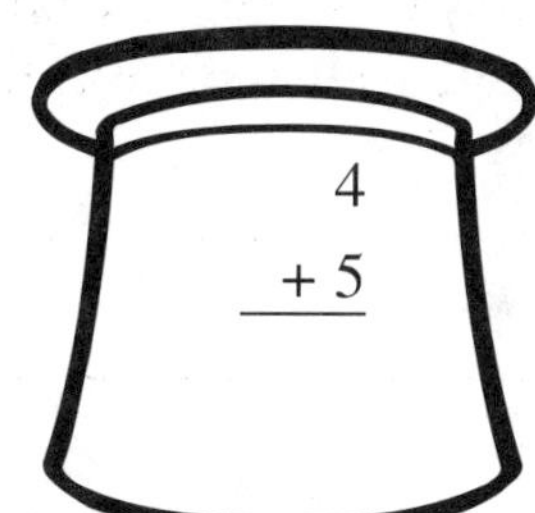


9. 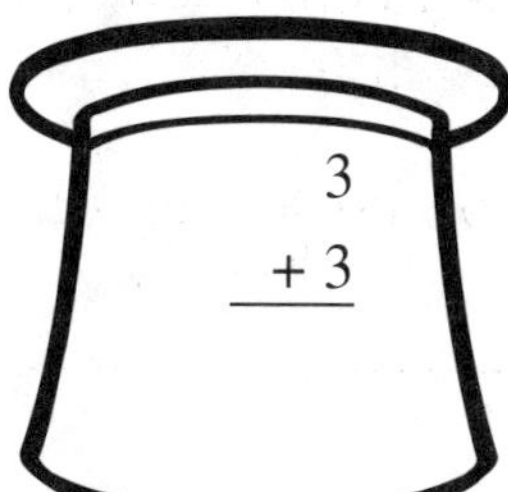


10. 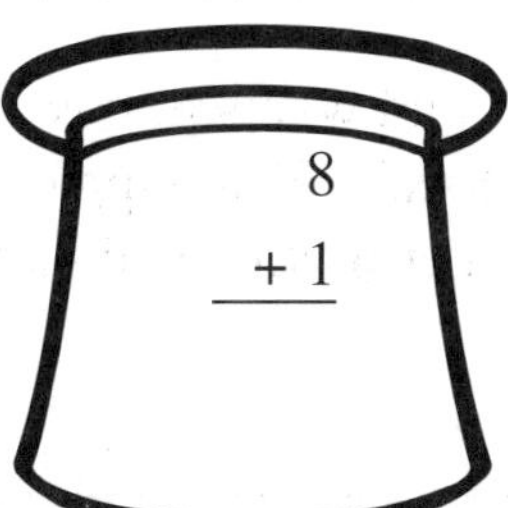


11. 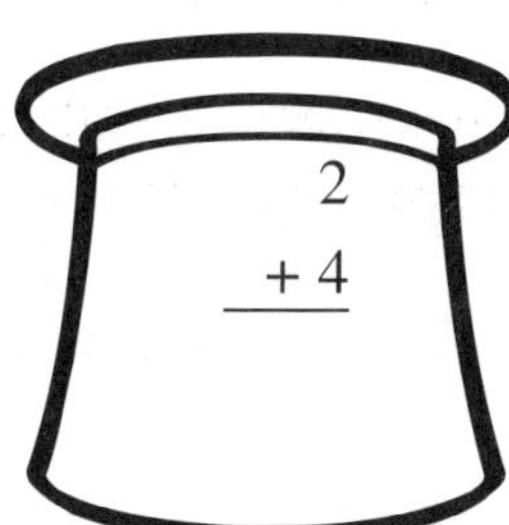


12. 

13. 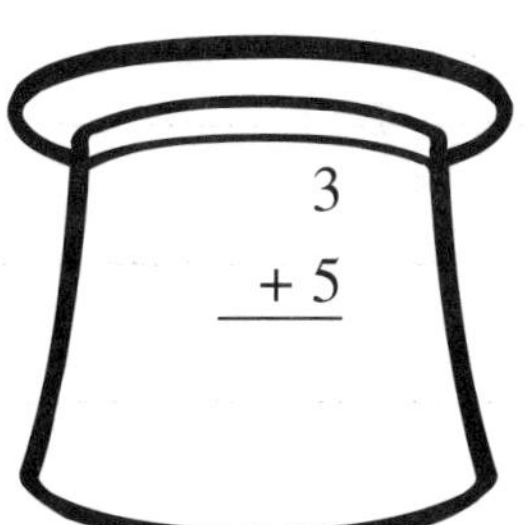


14. 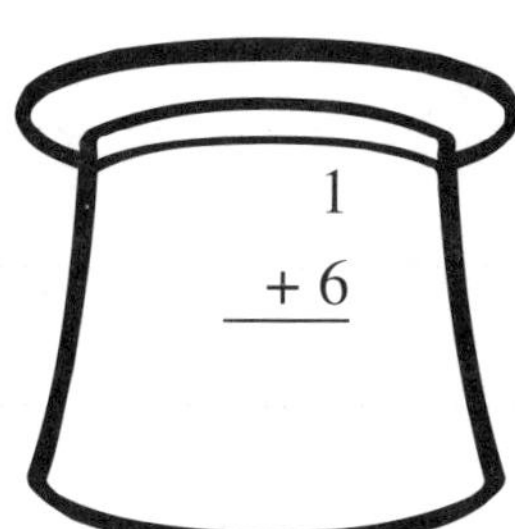


15. 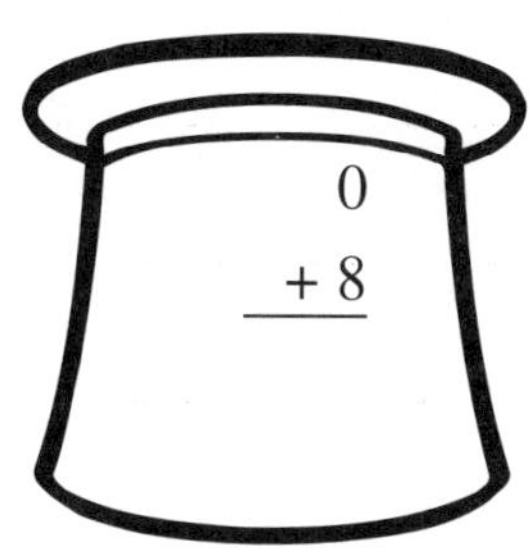

# Flip Jacks

If someone offered you five pancakes and one pancake would you want them? What if someone offered you one pancake and five pancakes? Would you want them? Which is more?

$$5 + 1 = 6$$

$$1 + 5 = 6$$

Flipping the numbers around in an addition problem does not change the answer.

**Directions:** Look at each addition problem. Add to find the answer.

1. $5 + 6 =$ ____ $6 + 5 =$ ____
2. $7 + 8 =$ ____ $8 + 7 =$ ____
3. $2 + 8 =$ ____ $8 + 2 =$ ____
4. $3 + 4 =$ ____ $4 + 3 =$ ____
5. $4 + 7 =$ ____ $7 + 4 =$ ____
6. $9 + 2 =$ ____ $2 + 9 =$ ____
7. $3 + 1 =$ ____ $1 + 3 =$ ____
8. $5 + 3 =$ ____ $3 + 5 =$ ____
9. $9 + 8 =$ ____ $8 + 9 =$ ____
10. $7 + 6 =$ ____ $6 + 7 =$ ____

 

# Do You Know?

**Directions:** Solve each problem by drawing dots or lines to represent each number. Add to find the sum. Circle the correct answer.

**Example:** 15 + 11 =

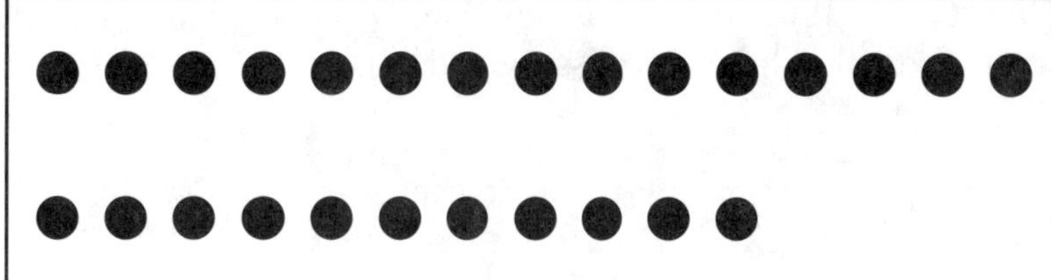

(A.) 26

B. 30

C. 4

D. 27

1. 18 + 9 =

   A. 23

   B. 26

   C. 9

   D. 27

2. 12 + 12 =

   A 24

   B. 12

   C. 26

   D. 0

3. 6 + 9 =

   A. 17

   B. 15

   C. 3

   D. 16

4. 20 + 8 =

   A. 30

   B. 18

   C. 12

   D. 28

5. 11 + 9 =

   A. 21

   B. 20

   C. 19

   D. 2

# Blooming Answers

Math answers are hidden in the flower garden. See if you can find the correct answers hidden inside the flowers.

**Directions:** Find the missing addend. Write the correct number on the line provided. Then, color only the flowers that have the missing addends.

1. _____ + 9 = 12 

2. 6 + _____ = 10 

3. 18 + _____ = 23 

4. 35 + _____ = 35 

5. 7 + _____ = 7 

1

6. _____ + 4 = 12 

7. _____ + 5 = 15 

8. 8 + _____ = 17 

9. _____ + 3 = 12 

10. _____ + 5 = 93 

4

# Dazzling Double Digits

**Directions:** Add each problem to find the answer.

1. 22 + 18
2. 34 + 16
3. 62 + 39
4. 15 + 17
5. 18 + 14
6. 21 + 19
7. 26 + 55
8. 83 + 17
9. 61 + 19
10. 43 + 28
11. 44 + 27
12. 66 + 24
13. 16 + 15
14. 54 + 28
15. 23 + 19
16. 22 + 10
17. 12 + 10
18. 18 + 13
19. 43 + 21
20. 19 + 17
21. 50 + 33

# Triple the Fun

*Part I*

**Directions:** Add the three-digit numbers to find the answer.

1. 309 + 208 = ______
2. 128 + 222 = ______
3. 672 + 109 = ______
4. 111 + 119 = ______
5. 775 + 127 = ______
6. 222 + 219 = ______
7. 543 + 318 = ______
8. 345 + 425 = ______
9. 467 + 314 = ______

*Part II*

**Directions:** Solve the word problems.

10. Braliegh had 712 pennies. Her friend Serame gave her 157 more pennies. How many pennies did Braliegh have in all? ________________

11. Ella had perfect attendance for 179 days. Gage had perfect attendance for 170 days. All together how many total days of perfect attendance did they have? ________________

12. Anna had 213 baseball cards. Her brother gave her his entire collection of 709 cards. How many cards did Anna have in her collection then? ________________

# Going Down!

*Part I*

**Directions:** Add the columns to find the correct answer.

1. 8
   14
   + 45

2. 12
   66
   + 21

3. 17
   81
   + 13

4. 48
   17
   + 22

5. 52
   37
   + 6

6. 90
   8
   + 12

7. 78
   10
   + 2

8. 43
   13
   + 51

9. 32
   9
   + 75

*Part II*

**Directions:** Add to find the answers.

10. 7 + 23 + 18 = ________________

11. 87 + 10 + 5 = ________________

12. 20 + 30 + 40 = ________________

13. 15 + 25 + 35 = ________________

14. 12 + 24 + 7 = ________________

15. 51 + 60 + 3 = ________________

16. 33 + 33 + 33 = ________________

17. 84 + 2 + 10 = ________________

18. 98 + 10 + 2 = ________________

19. 62 + 11 + 22 = ________________

# Putting the Dot in the Right Spot

When you add numbers with decimals be sure to put the decimal in the right spot.

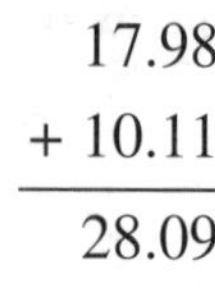

$$\begin{array}{r} 17.98 \\ +\ 10.11 \\ \hline 28.09 \end{array}$$

Notice the decimal stays in the same place.

**Directions:** Add each problem. Be sure to include the decimal.

1. $\begin{array}{r} 11.23 \\ +\ 10.11 \\ \hline \end{array}$

2. $\begin{array}{r} 16.78 \\ +\ 12.12 \\ \hline \end{array}$

3. $\begin{array}{r} 98.12 \\ +\ 1.10 \\ \hline \end{array}$

4. $\begin{array}{r} 20.02 \\ +\ 2.02 \\ \hline \end{array}$

5. $\begin{array}{r} 15.7 \\ +\ 13.9 \\ \hline \end{array}$

6. $\begin{array}{r} 14.2 \\ +\ 2.6 \\ \hline \end{array}$

7. $\begin{array}{r} 72.1 \\ +\ 2.5 \\ \hline \end{array}$

8. $\begin{array}{r} 6.3 \\ +\ 1.8 \\ \hline \end{array}$

9. $\begin{array}{r} 9.88 \\ +\ 1.21 \\ \hline \end{array}$

10. $\begin{array}{r} 8.99 \\ +\ 2.21 \\ \hline \end{array}$

11. $\begin{array}{r} 23.2 \\ +\ 17.3 \\ \hline \end{array}$

12. $\begin{array}{r} 17.89 \\ +\ 16.11 \\ \hline \end{array}$

13. $\begin{array}{r} 7.21 \\ +\ 6.21 \\ \hline \end{array}$

14. $\begin{array}{r} 33.45 \\ +\ 14.44 \\ \hline \end{array}$

15. $\begin{array}{r} 87.01 \\ +\ 12.22 \\ \hline \end{array}$

16. $\begin{array}{r} 22.22 \\ +\ 11.11 \\ \hline \end{array}$

17. $\begin{array}{r} 77.87 \\ +\ 18.78 \\ \hline \end{array}$

18. $\begin{array}{r} 64.46 \\ +\ 46.64 \\ \hline \end{array}$

 

# Just Warming Up

*Part I*

**Directions:** Subtract to find the answer.

1. 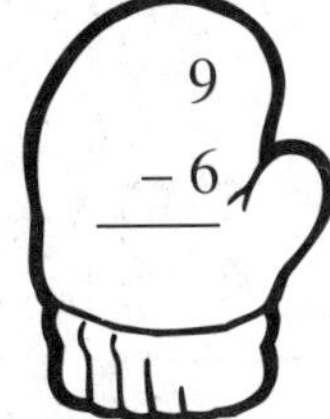


2. 

3. 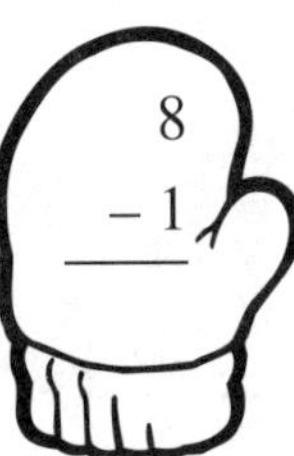


4. 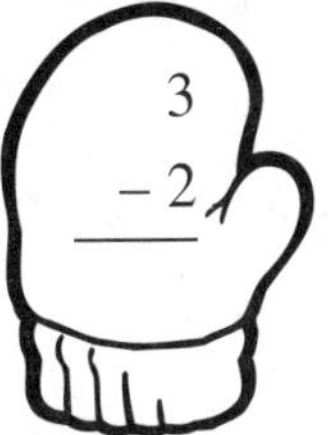


5. 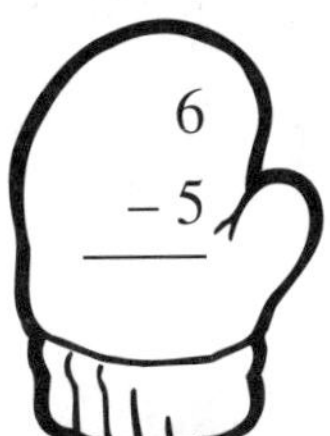


6. 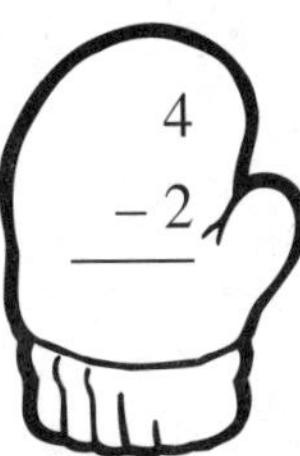


7. 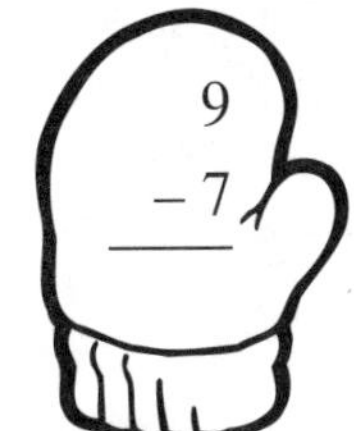


8. 

9. 

10. 

11. 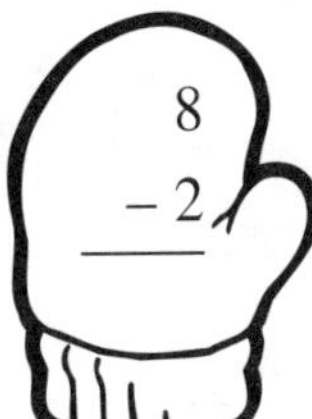


12. 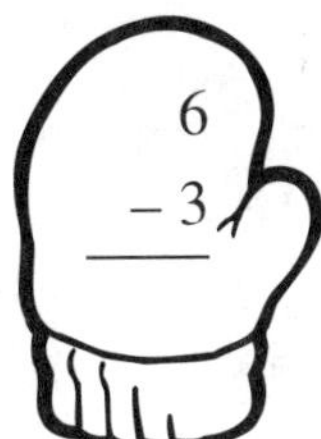


*Part II*

**Directions:** Subtract to find the answer.

13. 8 – 5 = ______________________________

14. 6 – 4 = ______________________________

15. 7 – 3 = ______________________________

16. 4 – 1 = ______________________________

17. 5 – 2 = ______________________________

18. 3 – 3 = ______________________________

19. 9 – 6 = ______________________________

20. 8 – 3 = ______________________________

# Subtraction Reaction

**Directions:** Subtract to find each answer. If the answer is greater than 50, draw a smiley face beside the answer. If the answer is less than 50, draw a frowning face beside the answer.

1. 88 − 14 = ☐
2. 21 − 10 = ☐
3. 76 − 19 = ☐
4. 65 − 18 = ☐
5. 77 − 12 = ☐
6. 40 − 33 = ☐
7. 86 − 17 = ☐
8. 51 − 23 = ☐
9. 99 − 33 = ☐

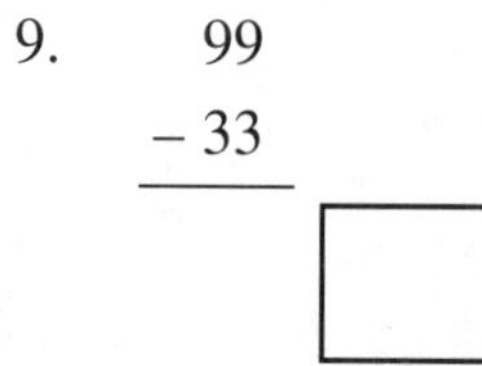

10. 75 − 25 = ☐
11. 26 − 13 = ☐
12. 17 − 16 = ☐

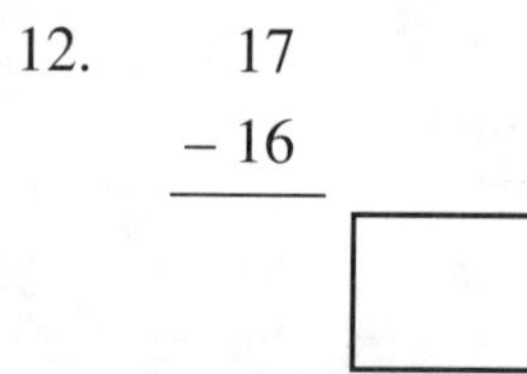

13. 50 − 48 = ☐
14. 39 − 29 = ☐
15. 87 − 77 = ☐

In the space below, create and answer four subtraction problems of your own. Remember to draw a smiley or frowning face beside your answer.

16. ______ + ______ = ☐
17. ______ + ______ = ☐
18. ______ + ______ = ☐
19. ______ + ______ = ☐

 

# Take Away

*Part I*

**Directions:** Complete each equation.

1. 35 – _______ = 7
2. 18 – _______ = 9
3. _______ – 2 = 18
4. 76 – _______ = 33
5. 89 – _______ = 32
6. 900 – _______ = 400
7. _______ – 356 = 0
8. 49 – _______ = 7
9. 100 – _______ = 50
10. _______ – 6 = 6

*Part II*

**Directions:** Subtract to find the answer.

11. 55 – 22 = ____
12. 98 – 43 = ____
13. 43 – 12 = ____
14. 76 – 45 = ____
15. 78 – 20 = ____
16. 44 – 17 = ____
17. 85 – 40 = ____
18. 30 – 15 = ____
19. 21 – 11 = ____
20. 66 – 33 = ____
21. 12 – 2 = ____
22. 90 – 45 = ____

# Right on Target

**Directions:** Solve each subtraction problem to hit the center of the target.

1. 754 − 135
2. 888 − 777
3. 721 − 432
4. 312 − 289
5. 211 − 101
6. 621 − 403
7. 110 − 100
8. 389 − 299
9. 498 − 150
10. 923 − 554
11. 117 − 117
12. 827 − 236
13. 909 − 181
14. 131 − 121
15. 620 − 559

 

# Practice, Practice, Practice

**Directions:** Subtract to find the correct answer.

| | | |
|---|---|---|
| 1. 431 − 219 | 2. 786 − 354 | 3. 871 − 444 |
| 4. 761 − 321 | 5. 647 − 456 | 6. 321 − 201 |
| 7. 987 − 625 | 8. 651 − 412 | 9. 777 − 563 |
| 10. 679 − 324 | 11. 411 − 346 | 12. 983 − 890 |
| 13. 781 − 708 | 14. 677 − 667 | 15. 156 − 121 |
| 16. 475 − 129 | 17. 390 − 187 | 18. 290 − 117 |
| 19. 601 − 501 | 20. 290 − 190 | 21. 195 − 183 |
| 22. 486 − 412 | 23. 764 − 378 | 24. 905 − 598 |

# Word Problem Subtraction

**Directions:** Solve each word problem. Be sure to show your work.

1. Mrs. Willis has 33 students in her morning class. Her afternoon class has 18 students. How many more students does she have in the morning than in the afternoon?

   ____________________

2. The annual Turtle Derby is next Saturday. There are 52 turtles entered in the race. The committee hoped to have 78 turtles in the race. How many more turtles do they need to reach their goal?

   ____________________

3. Mr. Mackey runs the local candy shop. Last year he sold 700 candy bars in his shop. This year he has already sold 950 candy bars. How many more candy bars has he sold this year than last year?

   ____________________

4. Sophie and her brother Jake opened a lemonade stand. Sophie sold 57 glasses of lemonade by the end of the day. Jake turned his lemonade into lemonade popsicles. By the end of the day Jake had sold 88 lemonade popsicles. How many more lemonade products did Jake sell than Sophie?

   ____________________

5. Sammy Squirrel has been putting away acorns all winter long. He has 967 acorns for the long, cold winter. Sammy's cousin, Charlie Chipmunk, has only 200 acorns tucked away in his house. How many more acorns does Sammy have for the winter months than Charlie?

   ____________________

In the space below write a subtraction word problem of your own. Be sure to solve your problem when you are finished.

______________________________________________________________________

______________________________________________________________________

______________________________________________________________________

______________________________________________________________________

# Adding and Multiplying Go Hand in Hand

**Directions:** Complete each pair of number sentences. Write your answers in the hands.

1. 4 + 4 + 4 + 4 = 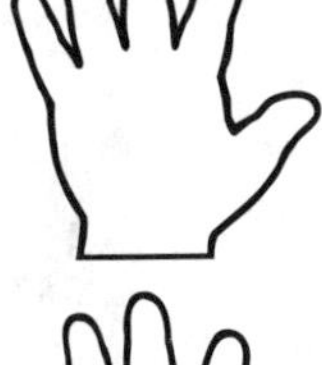 4 x 4 =

2. 5 + 5 + 5 + 5 + 5 =  5 x 5 =

3. 6 + 6 + 6 =  6 x 3 =

4. 2 + 2 + 2 + 2 + 2 + 2 =  2 x 6 =

5. 8 + 8 =  8 x 2 =

6. 1 + 1 + 1 + 1 + 1 + 1 + 1 =  1 x 7 =

7. 3 + 3 + 3 =  3 x 3 =

8. 7 + 7 + 7 + 7 =  7 x 4 =

# 3...2...1...Blast Off!

**Directions:** Multiply to find the answer.

1. 3 x 1 = ____________

2. 2 x 2 = ____________

3. 2 x 3 = ____________

4. 1 x 9 = ____________

5. 3 x 7 = ____________

6. 2 x 8 = ____________

7. 1 x 6 = ____________

8. 2 x 5 = ____________

9. 3 x 6 = ____________

10. 3 x 8 = ____________

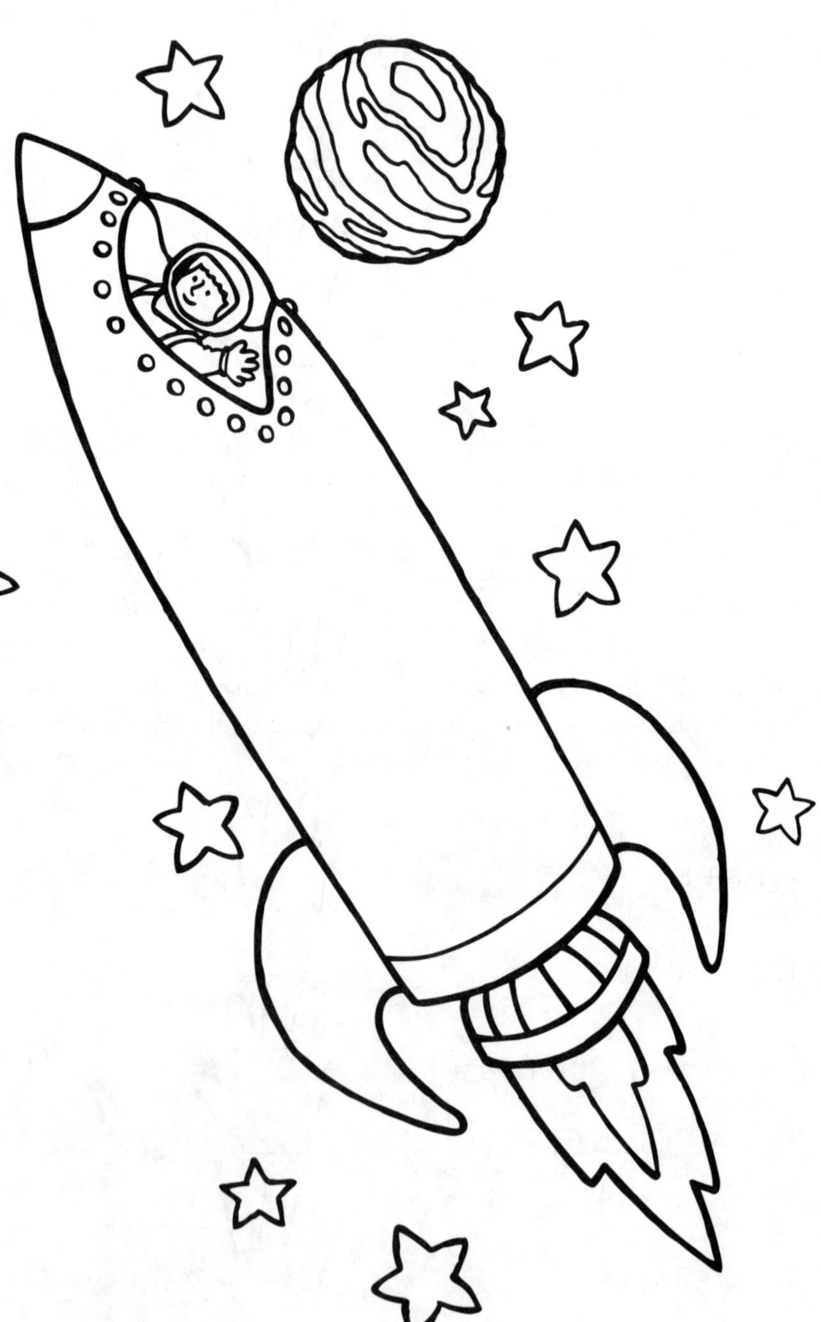

 

# More with Multiplication

**Directions:** Answer these multiplication problems with 4, 5, and 6 as factors.

1. 4 x 4 = ____________________
2. 5 x 5 = ____________________
3. 6 x 6 = ____________________
4. 4 x 0 = ____________________
5. 5 x 0 = ____________________
6. 6 x 0 = ____________________
7. 4 x 3 = ____________________
8. 5 x 3 = ____________________
9. 6 x 3 = ____________________
10. 4 x 7 = ____________________
11. 5 x 7 = ____________________
12. 6 x 7 = ____________________
13. 4 x 10 = ____________________
14. 5 x 10 = ____________________
15. 6 x 10 = ____________________
16. 4 x 8 = ____________________
17. 5 x 8 = ____________________
18. 6 x 8 = ____________________
19. 4 x 2 = ____________________
20. 5 x 2 = ____________________
21. 6 x 2 = ____________________
22. 4 x 5 = ____________________
23. 5 x 5 = ____________________
24. 6 x 5 = ____________________
25. 4 x 9 = ____________________
26. 5 x 9 = ____________________
27. 6 x 9 = ____________________
28. 4 x 12 = ____________________
29. 5 x 12 = ____________________
30. 6 x 12 = ____________________

# Learning Your Times: 7, 8, and 9

**Directions:** Multiply to find each product.

1. 7 x 1 = ___
2. 8 x 7 = ___
3. 7 x 3 = ___
4. 9 x 6 = ___
5. 9 x 0 = ___
6. 7 x 6 = ___
7. 8 x 3 = ___
8. 7 x 2 = ___
9. 8 x 9 = ___
10. 7 x 4 = ___
11. 9 x 2 = ___
12. 7 x 8 = ___
13. 9 x 3 = ___
14. 7 x 5 = ___
15. 8 x 6 = ___
16. 9 x 10 = ___
17. 8 x 12 = ___
18. 9 x 11 = ___
19. 8 x 8 = ___
20. 7 x 7 = ___

 

# Going to the Dogs

**Directions:** Solve each multiplication problem. If the product is greater than 70, color the dog nearest the problem. If the product is less than 70, then draw an X on the dog nearest the problem.

# Multiplication Trail

**Directions:** Follow the path from home to school to get you through the multiplication review.

# Beginning to Understand Division

When you divide things, you try to put them into equal groups. If you have 6 blocks, you can divide them into 2 groups of 3 or 3 groups of 2.

However, some numbers do not divide evenly. If you have 7 blocks you can divide them into 2 groups of 3 or 3 groups of 2 but in both cases you would have 1 block left over. This extra number in division is called a *remainder*.

**Directions:** Divide each set into two equal groups by drawing a box around each group. If there is a remainder, circle the remainder

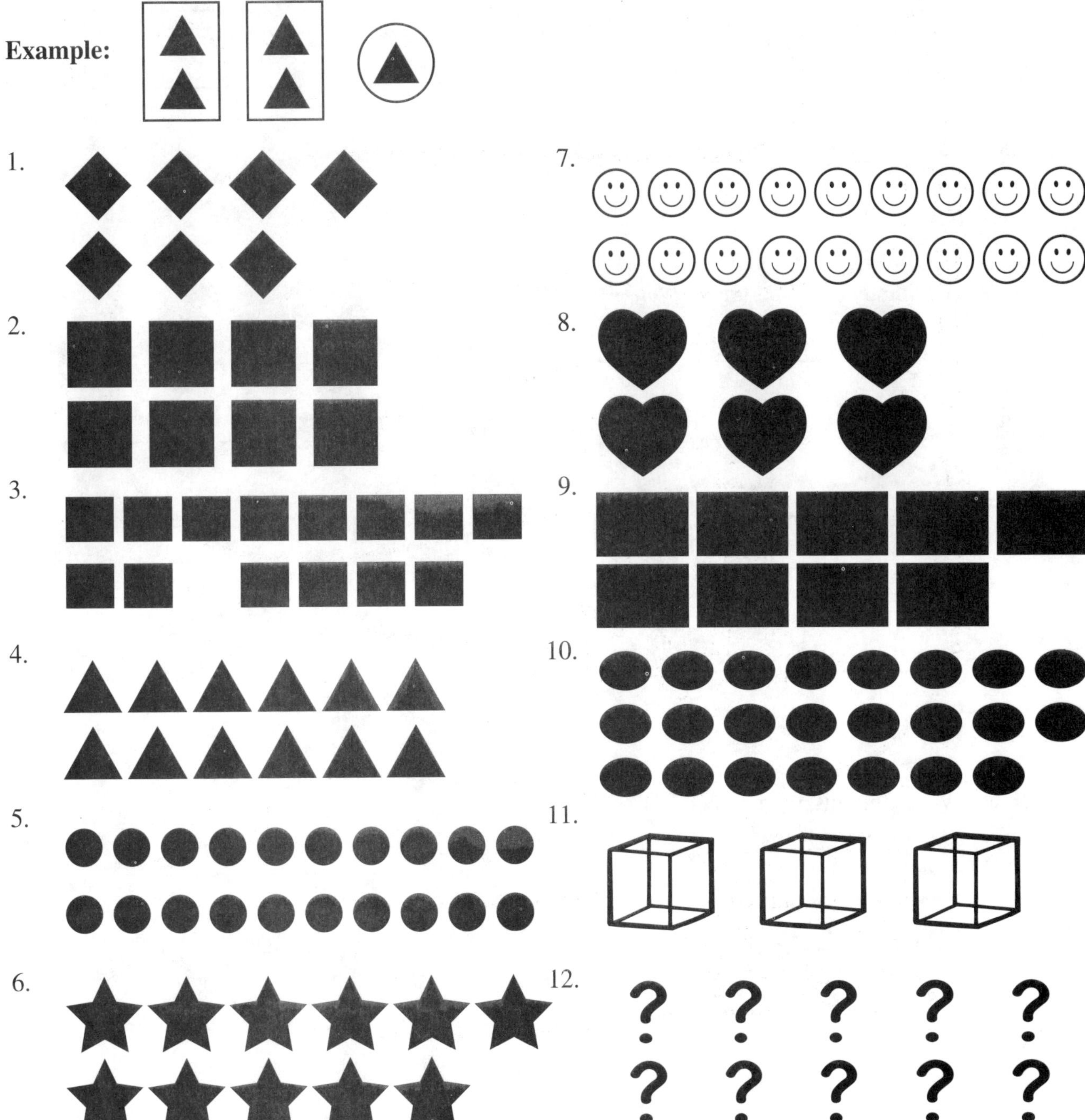

# Dividing with 2s and 3s

*Part I*

**Directions:** Divide by 2 to find the answer.

1. 18 ÷ 2 = ________________
2. 10 ÷ 2 = ________________
3. 24 ÷ 2 = ________________
4. 8 ÷ 2 = ________________
5. 16 ÷ 2 = ________________
6. 20 ÷ 2 = ________________
7. 6 ÷ 2 = ________________
8. 14 ÷ 2 = ________________
9. 22 ÷ 2 = ________________

*Part II*

**Directions:** Divide by 3 to find the answer.

10. 9 ÷ 3 = ________________
11. 12 ÷ 3 = ________________
12. 24 ÷ 3 = ________________
13. 18 ÷ 3 = ________________
14. 21 ÷ 3 = ________________
15. 15 ÷ 3 = ________________
16. 6 ÷ 3 = ________________
17. 27 ÷ 3 = ________________
18. 33 ÷ 3 = ________________

*Part III*

**Directions:** Write the missing number.

19. 24 ÷ ________________ = 12
20. 30 ÷ ________________ = 10
21. 36 ÷ ________________ = 12
22. 12 ÷ ________________ = 6
23. 22 ÷ ________________ = 11
24. 8 ÷ ________________ = 4

# 4, 5, and 6...Learn Division Quack

**Directions:** Look at each division problem. If the problem is correct, color the duck. If the problem is not correct, draw an X on the duck.

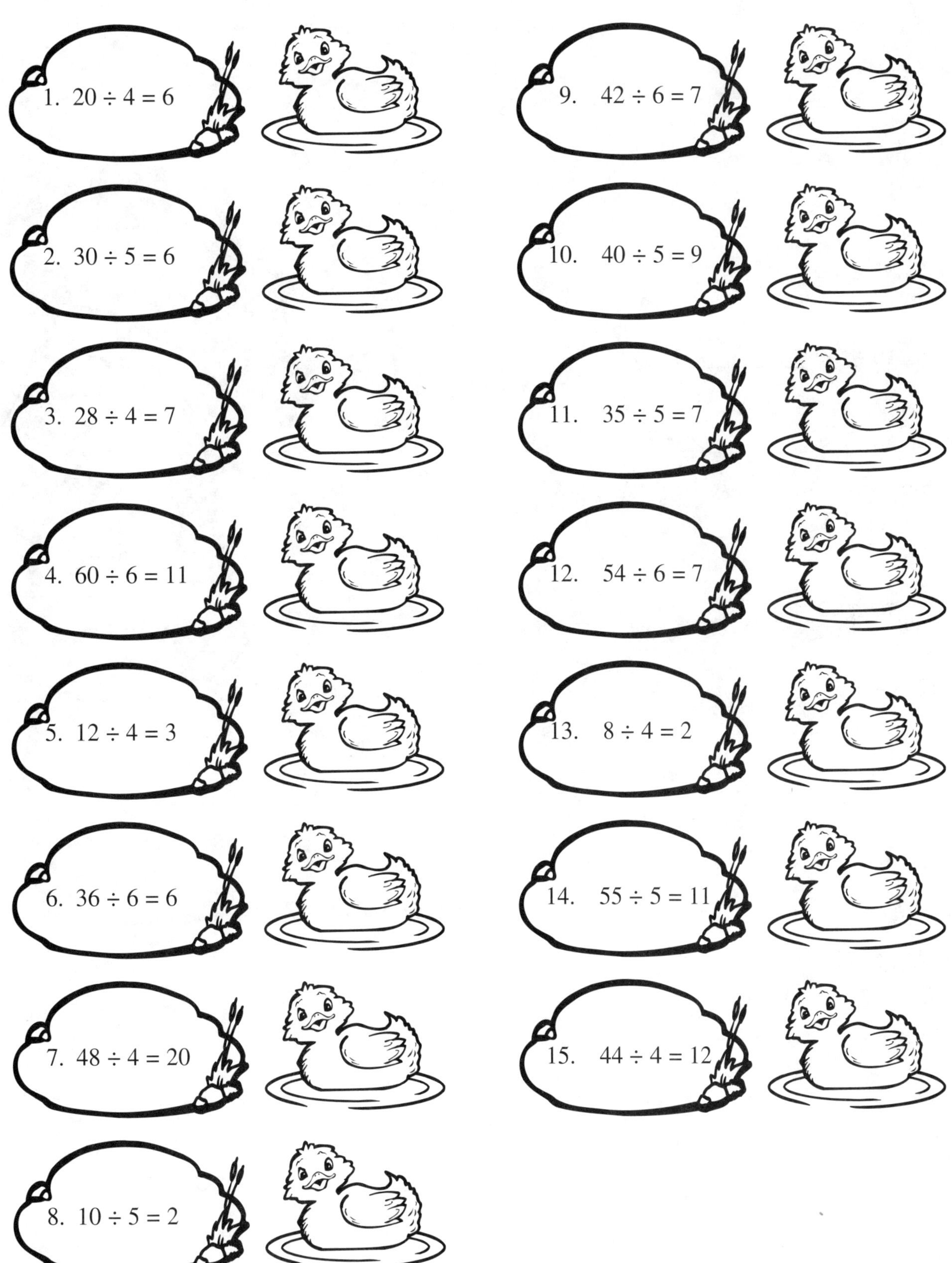

# 7, 8, and 9 — Solve the Riddle Every Time

**Directions:** Solve each division problem to find the hidden sentence below.

1. 21 ÷ 7 = __________ O
2. 16 ÷ 8 = __________ R
3. 81 ÷ 9 = __________ Y
4. 40 ÷ 8 = __________ U
5. 56 ÷ 8 = _________ M
6. 108 ÷ 9 = ________ S
7. 7 ÷ 7 = __________ A
8. 32 ÷ 8 = __________ A
9. 99 ÷ 9 = __________ T
10. 42 ÷ 7 = __________ E
11. 72 ÷ 9 = __________ R

| ___ | ___ | ___ | | ___ | ___ | ___ | | ___ | ___ | ___ | ___ | ___! |
|---|---|---|---|---|---|---|---|---|---|---|---|---|
| 9 | 3 | 5 | | 1 | 2 | 6 | | 12 | 7 | 4 | 8 | 11 |

 

# Double Digits...10, 11, and 12

**Directions:** Solve each division problem. Circle the correct answer.

1. 36 ÷ 12 =
   a. 13
   b. 3
   c. 2

2. 22 ÷ 11=
   a. 2
   b. 10
   c. 11

3. 100 ÷ 10 =
   a. 9
   b. 20
   c. 10

4. 121 ÷ 11 =
   a. 12
   b. 10
   c. 11

5. 48 ÷ 12 =
   a. 8
   b. 6
   c. 4

6. 33 ÷ 11 =
   a. 11
   b. 3
   c. 6

7. 60 ÷ 12 =
   a. 5
   b. 8
   c. 3

8. 70 ÷ 10 =
   a. 10
   b. 11
   c. 7

9. 55 ÷ 11 =
   a. 11
   b. 5
   c. 1

10. 24 ÷ 12 =
    a. 12
    b. 4
    c. 2

11. 20 ÷ 10 =
    a. 2
    b. 10
    c. 20

12. 110 ÷ 11 =
    a. 11
    b. 12
    c. 10

13. 96 ÷ 12 =
    a. 12
    b. 9
    c. 8

14. 77 ÷ 11 =
    a. 11
    b. 7
    c. 10

# Dividing and Multiplying Go Together

**Directions:** Complete each set of related problems.

1. 27 ÷ 3 = ____________ 3 x 9 = ____________
2. 12 ÷ 4 = ____________ 4 x 3 = ____________
3. 18 ÷ 6 = ____________ 6 x 3 = ____________
4. 10 ÷ 2 = ____________ 2 x 5 = ____________
5. 88 ÷ 11 = ____________ 11 x 8 = ____________
6. 45 ÷ 9 = ____________ 9 x 5 = ____________
7. 7 ÷ 1 = ____________ 1 x 7 = ____________
8. 28 ÷ 4 = ____________ 4 x 7 = ____________
9. 36 ÷ 3 = ____________ 3 x 12 = ____________
10. 60 ÷ 10 = ____________ 10 x 6 = ____________
11. 44 ÷ 4 = ____________ 4 x 11 = ____________
12. 24 ÷ 6 = ____________ 6 x 4 = ____________
13. 50 ÷ 5 = ____________ 5 x 10 = ____________
14. 56 ÷ 8 = ____________ 8 x 7 = ____________
15. 14 ÷ 2 = ____________ 2 x 7 = ____________
16. 48 ÷ 4 = ____________ 4 x 12 = ____________

# Which One's Right?

**Directions:** Divide each problem. Be sure to show your work. Then, circle the correct answer.

1. $2\overline{)140}$
   a. 140
   b. 17
   c. 70
   d. 40

2. $3\overline{)180}$
   a. 16
   b. 60
   c. 90
   d. 18

3. $4\overline{)28}$
   a. 7
   b. 6
   c. 4
   d. 12

4. $11\overline{)121}$
   a. 10
   b. 12
   c. 11
   d. 15

5. $9\overline{)360}$
   a. 4
   b. 14
   c. 36
   d. 40

6. $2\overline{)222}$
   a. 111
   b. 22
   c. 12
   d. 120

7. $7\overline{)490}$
   a. 70
   b. 17
   c. 60
   d. 80

8. $8\overline{)560}$
   a. 170
   b. 56
   c. 70
   d. 80

# Quick Division

*Part I*

**Directions:** Find the answer to each division problem.

1. $50 \div 10 =$ ____________
2. $60 \div 6 =$ ____________
3. $20 \div 2 =$ ____________
4. $55 \div 11 =$ ____________
5. $40 \div 2 =$ ____________
6. $80 \div 4 =$ ____________
7. $90 \div 9 =$ ____________
8. $100 \div 10 =$ ____________
9. $10 \div 2 =$ ____________
10. $30 \div 10 =$ ____________
11. $30 \div 3 =$ ____________
12. $88 \div 11 =$ ____________

*Part II*

**Directions:** Complete each equation.

13. ____________ $\div 10 = 70$
14. $100 \div$ ____________ $= 10$
15. $50 \div$ ____________ $= 5$
16. ____________ $\div 10 = 8$
17. $55 \div$ ____________ $= 11$
18. $20 \div$ ____________ $= 10$
19. ____________ $\div 10 = 4$
20. $30 \div$ ____________ $= 3$

 

# Patterns in Division

**Directions:** You can do long division problems quickly if you understand the pattern. Find the pattern for each set of division problems. Then divide to find the answer.

1. $2\overline{)4}$ $2\overline{)40}$ $2\overline{)400}$ $2\overline{)4{,}000}$

2. $2\overline{)6}$ $2\overline{)60}$ $2\overline{)600}$ $2\overline{)6{,}000}$

3. $7\overline{)28}$ $7\overline{)280}$ $7\overline{)2{,}800}$ $7\overline{)28{,}000}$

4. $1\overline{)6}$ $1\overline{)60}$ $1\overline{)600}$ $1\overline{)6{,}000}$

5. $4\overline{)20}$ $4\overline{)200}$ $4\overline{)2{,}000}$ $4\overline{)20{,}000}$

6. $3\overline{)9}$ $3\overline{)90}$ $3\overline{)900}$ $3\overline{)9{,}000}$

7. $5\overline{)5}$ $5\overline{)50}$ $5\overline{)500}$ $5\overline{)5{,}000}$

8. $8\overline{)32}$ $8\overline{)320}$ $8\overline{)3{,}200}$ $8\overline{)32{,}000}$

9. $6\overline{)12}$ $6\overline{)120}$ $6\overline{)1{,}200}$ $6\overline{)12{,}000}$

10. $9\overline{)18}$ $9\overline{)180}$ $9\overline{)1{,}800}$ $9\overline{)18{,}000}$

# And Some Left Over

Sometimes when you divide, the problem doesn't work out evenly. When this happens you have a remainder.

**Example:**

$$\begin{array}{r} 7 \text{ R2} \\ 6\overline{)44} \\ \underline{42} \\ 2 \end{array}$$

**Directions:** Divide each problem. Be sure to show your work.

1. $2\overline{)73}$
2. $4\overline{)75}$
3. $8\overline{)97}$
4. $9\overline{)98}$
5. $7\overline{)93}$
6. $6\overline{)62}$
7. $4\overline{)79}$
8. $2\overline{)57}$
9. $2\overline{)29}$
10. $4\overline{)15}$
11. $3\overline{)82}$
12. $6\overline{)73}$
13. $3\overline{)55}$
14. $6\overline{)15}$
15. $2\overline{)49}$
16. $7\overline{)17}$
17. $3\overline{)38}$
18. $5\overline{)74}$
19. $8\overline{)97}$
20. $9\overline{)63}$

**Directions:** Solve the following word problem.

21. Tucker has 89 pieces of bubble gum. He divides them between his brother Preston and himself. How may pieces will each boy get if the pieces are divided equally? Will there be any pieces remaining? ____________

# A Part of the Whole

A *fraction* is a part of a whole. If you had a pizza for dinner and the pizza was cut into 8 equal slices, each slice would represent $\frac{1}{8}$ of the pizza. It would take eight $\frac{1}{8}$'s to make a whole pizza.

**Directions:** Draw a line and match the correct picture with the fraction that represents the shaded part(s) of the picture.

1.  a. $\frac{1}{4}$

2. 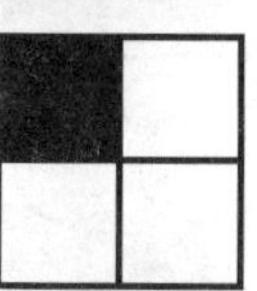 b. $\frac{4}{8}$

3.  c. $\frac{2}{3}$

4.  d. $\frac{1}{3}$

5.  e. $\frac{1}{2}$

6. 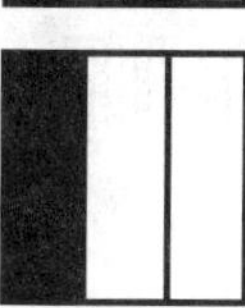 f. $\frac{3}{8}$

**Directions:** Read each fraction given and draw a picture to show that amount. **Hint:** It's easier to draw fractions using geometric shapes like circles, squares, and rectangles.

7. $\frac{1}{2}$ 8. $\frac{2}{5}$

9. $\frac{1}{6}$ 10. $\frac{4}{10}$

# A Part of the Group

A fraction can be used to name a part of a group. For example, pretend your friends are planning a trip to the movies. Of the five friends, three want to see a comedy but the other two want to go to a scary movie. This decision can be shown using fractions.

$\frac{3}{5}$ of your friends want to go to a comedy.

$\frac{2}{5}$ of your friends want to go to a scary movie.

**Directions:** Look at each group and write a fraction for the answer.

**Example:** How many of the stars have stripes?  $\frac{3}{5}$ have stripes.

1. What fraction of the circles have polka dots?  ____________

2. What fraction of the diamonds are shaded in? 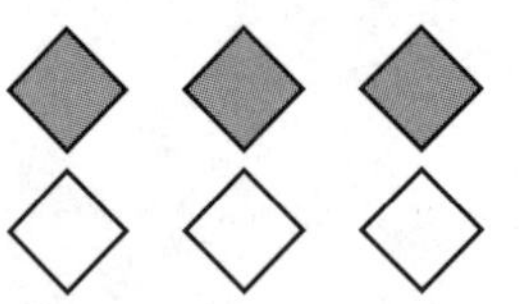 ____________

3. What fraction of the triangles are shaded in? ____________

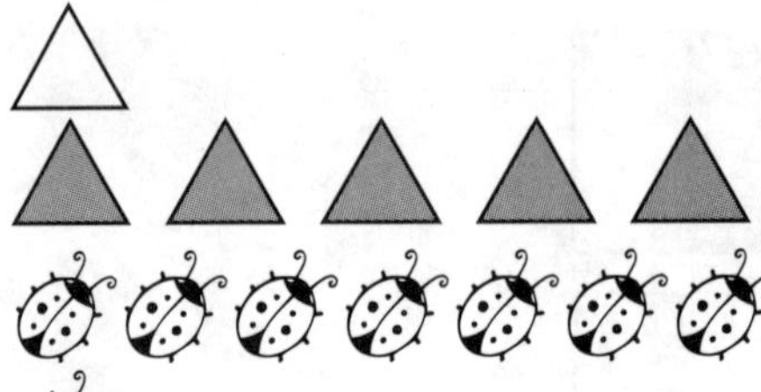

4. What fraction of the ladybugs have dots? ____________

5. What fraction of the squares have stripes? 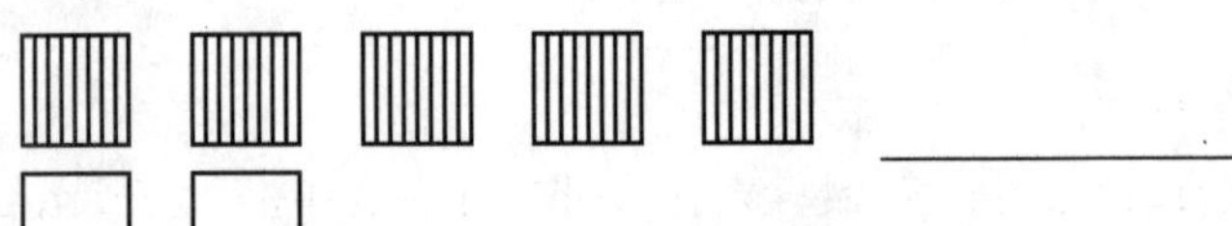 ____________

6. What fraction of the ants are shaded in?  ____________

7. What fraction of the circles have smiley faces?  ____________

8. What fraction of the squares are shaded in? 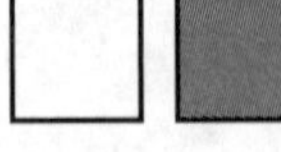 ____________

# Adding and Subtracting Fractions

When the bottom numbers of fractions are the same, those fractions can be added or subtracted.

$\frac{1}{4} + \frac{2}{4} = \frac{3}{4}$ and $\frac{3}{4} - \frac{1}{4} = \frac{2}{4}$

Notice that the bottom number (the denominator) stays the same—only the top number (the numerator) changes.

*Part I*

**Directions:** Add the following fractions.

1. $\frac{2}{5} + \frac{3}{5} =$ ________________
2. $\frac{1}{8} + \frac{4}{8} =$ ________________
3. $\frac{1}{3} + \frac{1}{3} =$ ________________
4. $\frac{2}{6} + \frac{3}{6} =$ ________________
5. $\frac{1}{4} + \frac{3}{4} =$ ________________
6. $\frac{4}{10} + \frac{3}{10} =$ ________________

*Part II*

**Directions:** Subtract the following fractions.

7. $\frac{4}{8} - \frac{1}{8} =$ ________________
8. $\frac{5}{6} - \frac{2}{6} =$ ________________
9. $\frac{7}{10} - \frac{3}{10} =$ ________________
10. $\frac{3}{4} - \frac{2}{4} =$ ________________
11. $\frac{3}{3} - \frac{2}{3} =$ ________________
12. $\frac{8}{9} - \frac{6}{9} =$ ________________

*Part III*

**Directions:** Solve each problem and draw a picture to represent the answer.

13. $\frac{2}{3} + \frac{1}{3} =$ ________________

14. $\frac{2}{6} - \frac{1}{6} =$ ________________

# Probable Probability

Remember that probability can be written as a fraction. Suppose you have three friends—Jack, Sarah, and Candy—who usually call you. The phone rings early on Saturday morning, and your mother answers it. She tells you the phone is for you and that it is one of your friends. What is the probability of answering the phone and finding out that it is Jack who has called you?

The probability of Jack being on the line is 1 in 3 or $\frac{1}{3}$.

**Directions:** Read each problem. Circle the correct answer.

1. Four balls are placed in a box. One is red, one is green, one is yellow, and one is blue. What is the probability of pulling a red ball from the box?

   a. $\frac{1}{3}$

   b. $\frac{2}{4}$

   c. $\frac{1}{4}$

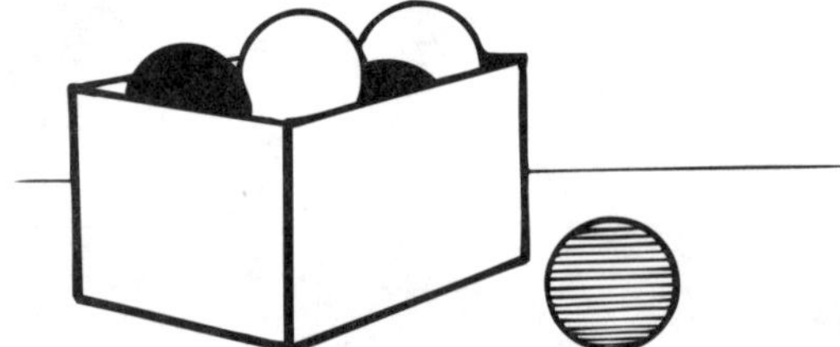

2. Two kittens are hiding under a chair. One kitten is a fluffy girl kitten. The other kitten is a fluffy boy kitten. What is the probability of the boy kitten coming out from under the chair first?

   a. $\frac{1}{3}$

   b. $\frac{1}{2}$

   c. $\frac{2}{3}$

3. A magician puts two rabbits in a hat. One rabbit is black. One rabbit is brown. What is the probability of drawing the black rabbit out of the hat?

   a. $\frac{1}{2}$

   b. $\frac{1}{3}$

   c. $\frac{1}{4}$

4. Cade has four pairs of socks left in his drawer. One pair is white, one is black, one is tan, and one is green. If Cade reaches in his hand and without looking pulls out a pair of socks to wear, what is the probability that he will pull out the white pair?

   a. $\frac{1}{2}$

   b. $\frac{2}{4}$

   c. $\frac{1}{4}$

# Can You Find the Pattern?

*Part I*

**Directions:** Finding patterns is like solving puzzles. See if you can match the patterns below. Draw a line from each pattern on the left to its partner on the right.

| | |
|---|---|
| 1. up, down, up, | a. 40, 50, 60 |
| 2. 10, 20, 30, | b. W, V, U |
| 3. blue, red, red, | c. April, May, June |
| 4. 9, 18, 27, | d. ?, !, ? |
| 5. 20, 19, 18, | e. girl, boy, girl |
| 6. Z, Y, X, | f. 500, 400, 300 |
| 7. January, February, March, | g. 17, 16, 15 |
| 8. boy, girl, boy, | h. blue, red, red |
| 9. 800, 700, 600, | i. 36, 45, 54 |
| 10. !, ?, !, | j. down, up, down |

*Part II*

**Directions:** Complete each pattern.

11. 10 x 10, 11 x 11, 12 x 12, __________, __________, __________

12. ABC, DEF, GHI, __________, __________, __________

13. 1, 22, 333, __________, __________, __________

14. 25, 40, 55, __________, __________, __________

15. 1/4, 1/5, 1/6, __________, __________, __________

# Everywhere Area

*Area* is the number of square units in a particular space. To find the area of a shape, count the number of squares. The area for this figure is 11 square units.

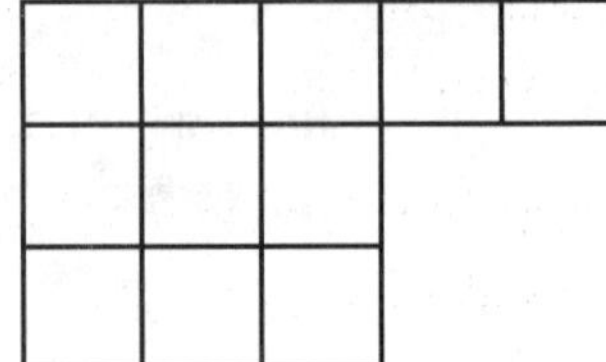

*Part I*

**Directions:** Find the area of each figure.

1. _______ square units

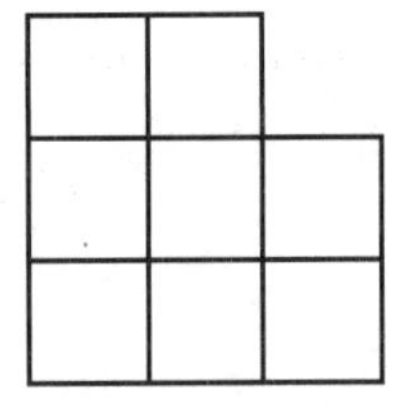

2. _______ square units

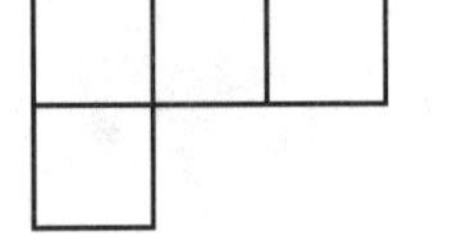

3. _______ square units

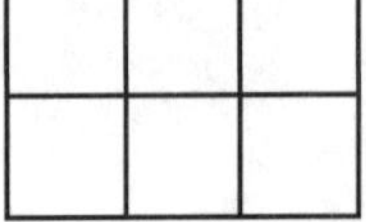

4. _______ square units

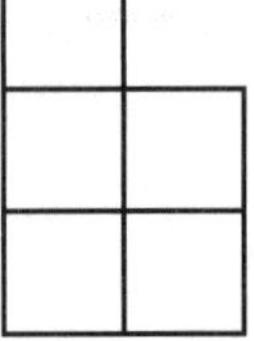

5. _______ square units

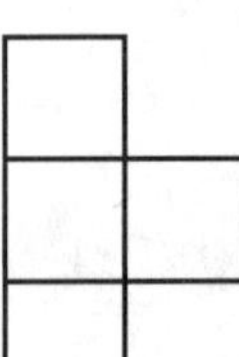

6. _______ square units

*Part II*

**Directions:** Draw a figure that has the number of square units given.

7. 8 square units

8. 12 square units

9. 2 square units

10. 9 square units

11. 14 square units

12. 15 square units

 

# Measuring the Temperature

In Canada and most other countries of the world, the Celsius scale is used. In the Celsius (or centigrade) scale, water freezes at 0 degrees and boils at 100 degrees at sea level.

In the United States, the Fahrenheit scale is used to measure temperature. In the Fahrenheit scale, water freezes at 32 degrees, and water boils at 210 degrees at sea level.

Here is a chart that compares some Fahrenheit and Celsius temperatures.

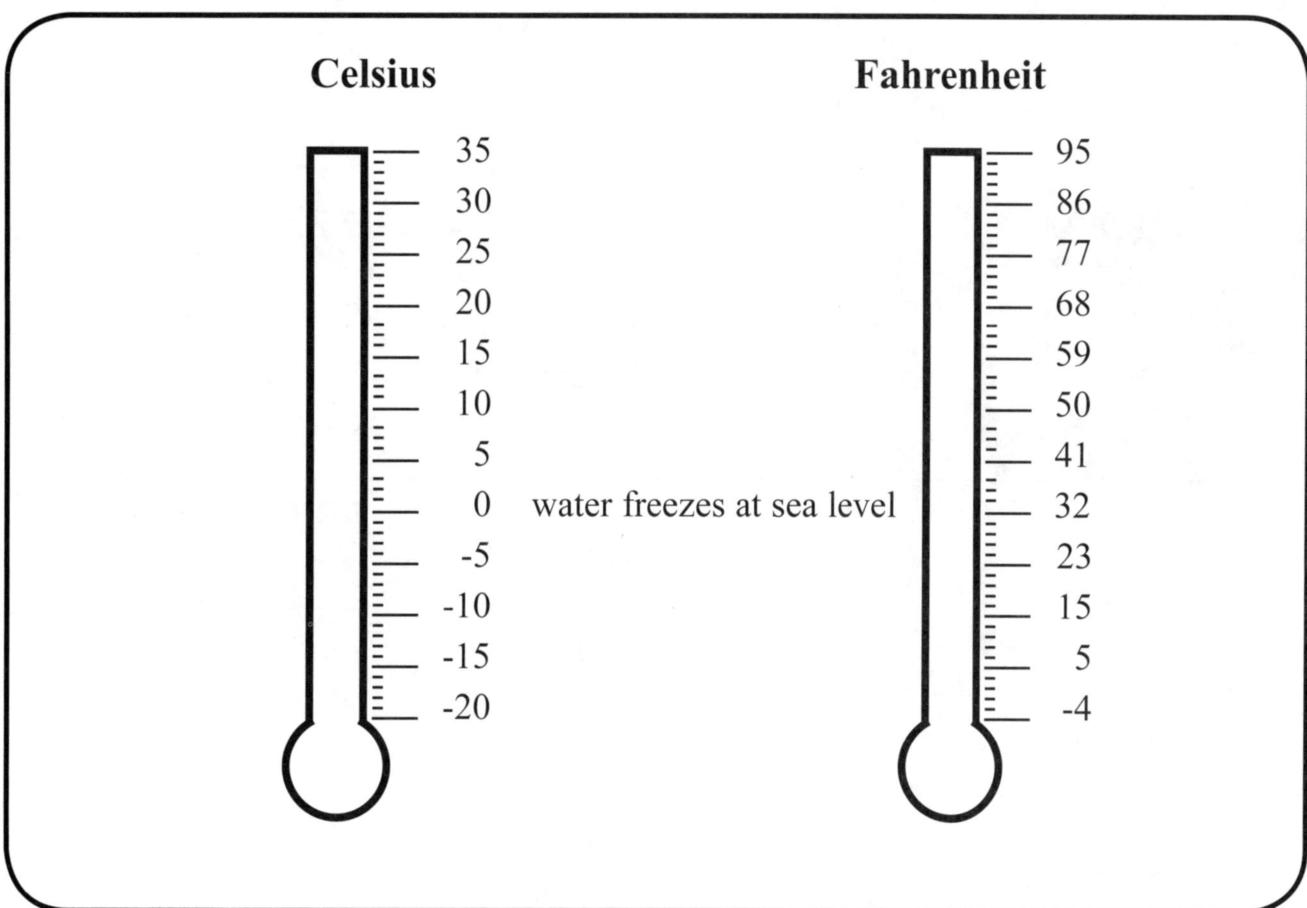


You can see that temperatures look lower using the Celsius scale. On the Fahrenheit scale, 35 degrees would be very cold outside, but on the Celsius scale, it is very hot!

If the temperature changes by 10 degrees on the centrigrade scale, it changes by 18 degrees on the Fahrenheit scale.

# How Cold Is It?

Use the temperature chart on the page 103 to decide what temperature would be good for these activities. Compare your answers with other students in your class. Why would some people have different answers?

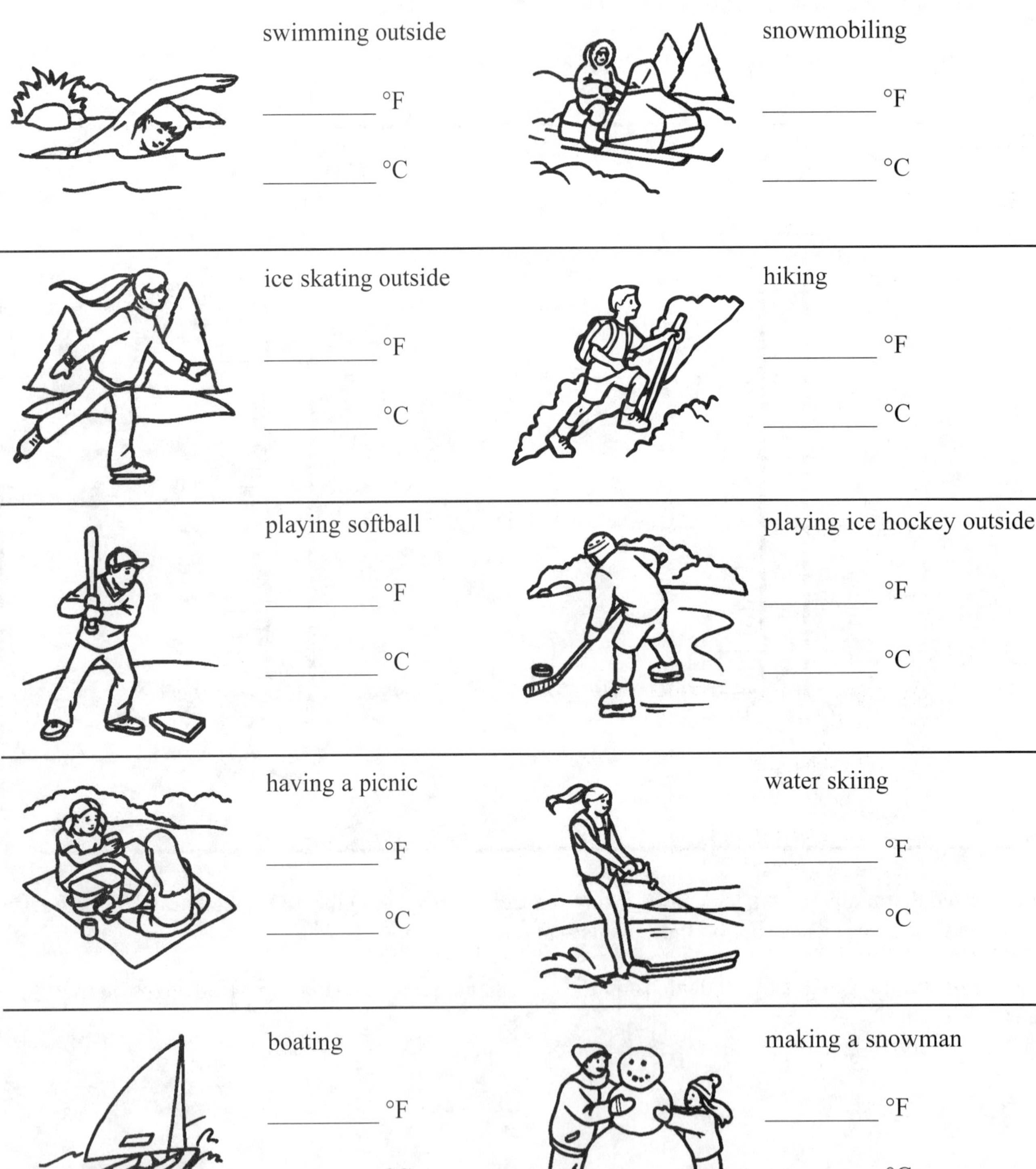

swimming outside

_________ °F

_________ °C

snowmobiling

_________ °F

_________ °C

ice skating outside

_________ °F

_________ °C

hiking

_________ °F

_________ °C

playing softball

_________ °F

_________ °C

playing ice hockey outside

_________ °F

_________ °C

having a picnic

_________ °F

_________ °C

water skiing

_________ °F

_________ °C

boating

_________ °F

_________ °C

making a snowman

_________ °F

_________ °C

 

# Measuring Length

*Centimeters* and *decimeters* are two units used for measuring length.

1 centimeter = 10 decimeters

*Part I*

**Directions:** Draw a line to match each item to the closest measurement.

1. 5 cm

2. 7 cm

3. 1 dm

*Part II*

**Directions:** Draw a picture of your own that matches each measurement. Use the back of your paper, if needed.

4. 4 centimeters
5. 1 decimeter
6. 1 centimeter
7. 2 decimeters
8. 6 centimeters

# Milliliters and Liters

*Milliliters* and *liters* are metric measurements. Milliliters are used to measure small amounts of liquid, and liters are used to measure larger amounts.

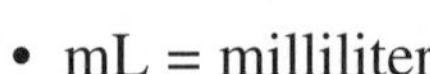

- mL = milliliter

- L = liter
- 1 liter = 1,000 milliliters

**Directions:** Choose the form you would use to measure each object. Circle the correct choice.

1. a bucket of water
   a. mL
   b. L
2. a glass of juice
   a. mL
   b. L
3. a pot of coffee
   a. mL
   b. L
4. a teaspoon of milk
   a. mL
   b. L
5. a pitcher of tea
   a. mL
   b. L
6. a laboratory beaker
   a. mL
   b. L
7. a child's swimming pool
   a. mL
   b. L
8. a mug of cider
   a. mL
   b. L
9. a dog's dish of water
   a. mL
   b. L
10. a baby's bottle
    a. mL
    b. L

 

# Ship Shape

**Directions:** Look at the picture of the ship. Find and color each shape listed below.

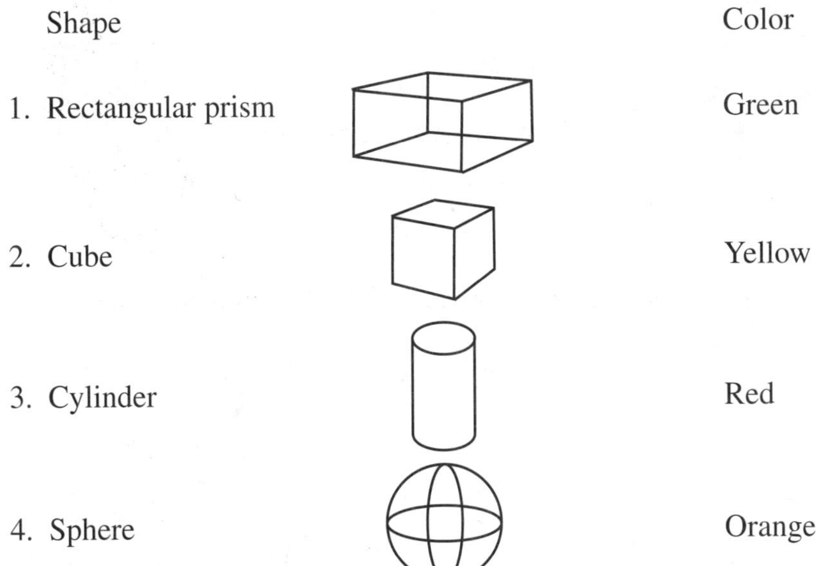

| Shape | Color |
|---|---|
| 1. Rectangular prism | Green |
| 2. Cube | Yellow |
| 3. Cylinder | Red |
| 4. Sphere | Orange |

**Something Extra:** Draw two cone shapes somewhere on your ship. Color the cones blue.

# Name the Shape

**Directions:** Name the shape of each figure. Choose from the list below.

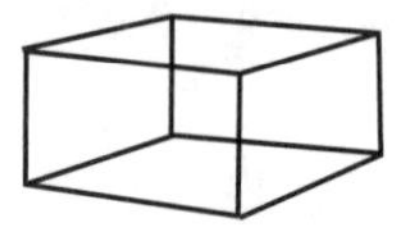
rectangular prism

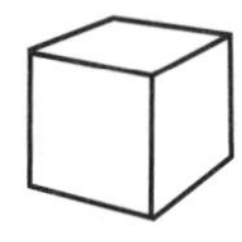
cube

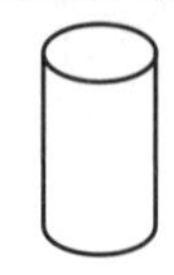
cylinder

sphere

cone

1. a witch's hat 
2. dice 
3. a shoe box 

4. a microwave oven 
5. a baseball 
6. an ice-cream cone 
7. a hat box 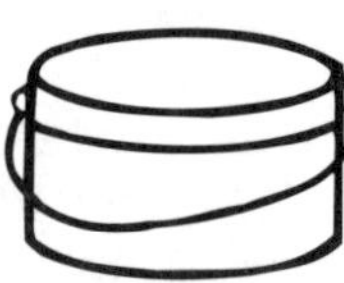
8. children's wooden blocks 
9. a can of soup 

10. a soccer ball 

Now it's your turn. In the spaces below, draw an example of each shape.

| sphere | cube | rectangular prism |
| --- | --- | --- |
| | | |

 

# Plane Figures

The outline of a shape forms a *plane figure*.

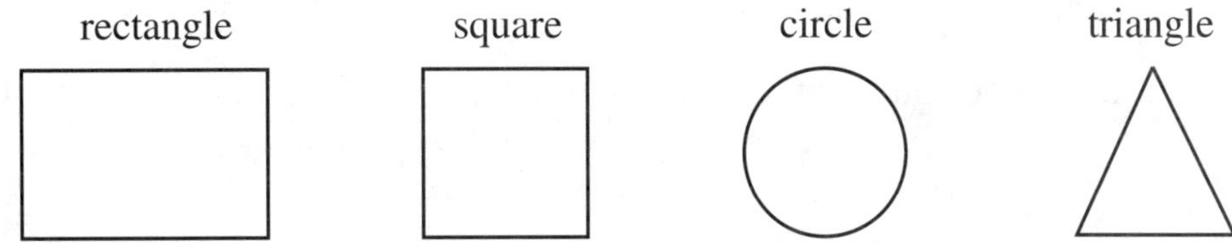


**Directions:** In the space below, draw a picture using only plane figures. Your shapes can be all different sizes. Be sure to color your picture when you are finished.

# Getting on Line

A *line* is straight with no end point. It goes on forever in both directions.

A *line segment* is straight and has two end points.

A *ray* is part of a line. It has one end point and the other end keeps going in one direction.

*Part I*

**Directions:** Circle the name of each figure.

1. ●———●
   a. line segment
   b. line
   c. ray
2. ●———►
   a. line segment
   b. line
   c. ray
3. ◄———●
   a. line segment
   b. line
   c. ray
4. ◄———►
   a. line segment
   b. line
   c. ray

*Part II*

**Directions:** Draw each picture.

5. Draw a sun with 10 rays.

6. Draw a house, using 6 to 8 line segments.

7. Draw a spider with 8 rays for legs.

 

# It's All in the Angle

Two rays with a common end point form an *angle*. The common end point is called a *vertex*. An angle that forms the shape of an L or a square corner is called a *right angle*.

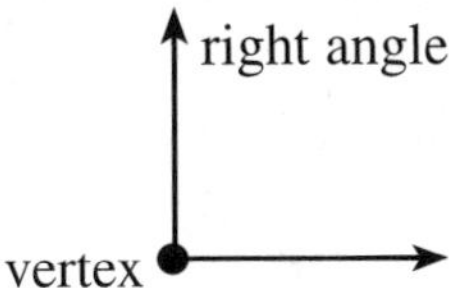


*Part I*

**Directions:** Look around the room. List at least 6 examples of right angles that you see.

**Example:** The corner of a fish tank.

1.

2.

3.

4.

5.

6.

*Part II*

**Directions:** Look at each figure. Write *yes* if the figure is an angle. Write *no* if the figure is not an angle.

7. __________

10. __________

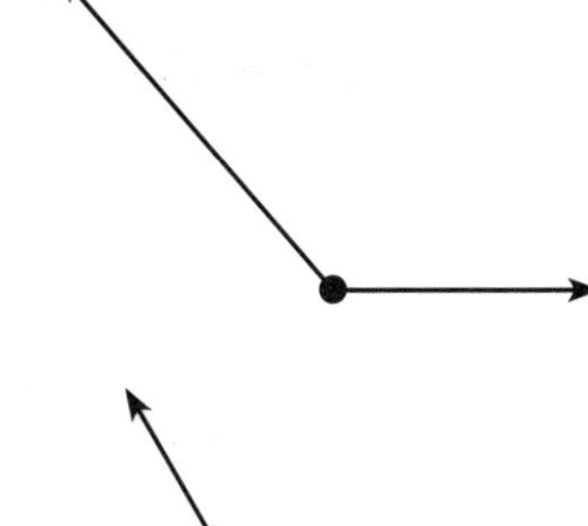

8. __________

11. __________

9. __________

12. __________

# It's All the Same

Figures that are *congruent* are the same size and shape. Congruent figures can be turned in any direction and still be congruent.

*Examples:* Congruent □□ ◇ Not Congruent □□

**Directions:** Use the graph below to draw eight sets of figures that are congruent.

# Congruent: Big Word, Easy Idea

When objects are *congruent* they are the same size and the same shape, no matter which way they are turned.

congruent squares squares that are not congruent

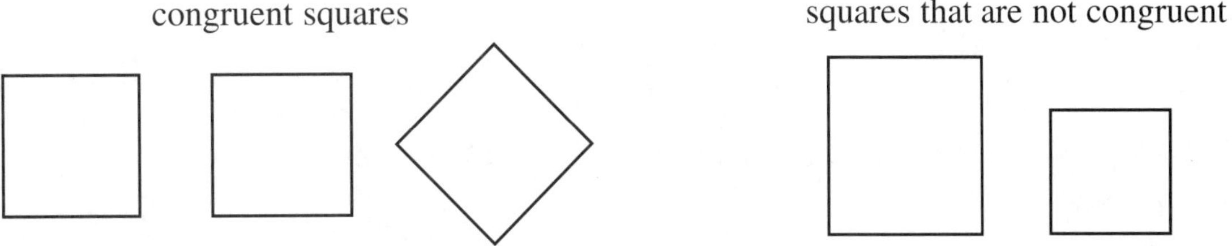

**Directions:** Look at the picture below. Find the 20 congruent shapes and color each of the 10 pairs the same color. Remember to change colors for each new pair.

# Perfect Symmetry

A *line of symmetry* divides a shape so that the two halves of the figure mirror each other across the line, like this.

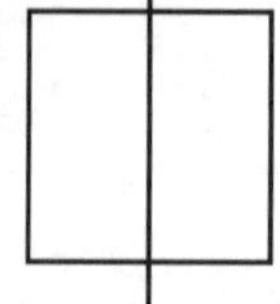

If you folded a shape along a line of symmetry, both sides would fit exactly together. Here are some symmetrical objects:

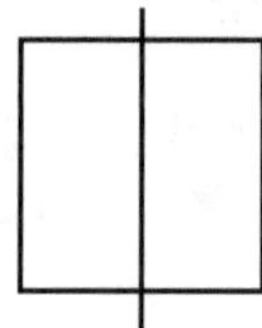
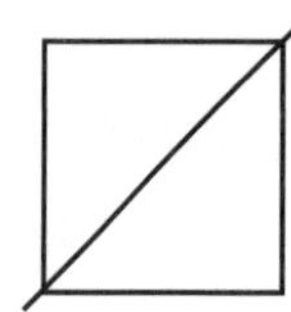

These objects are not symmetrical:

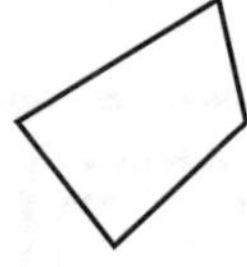
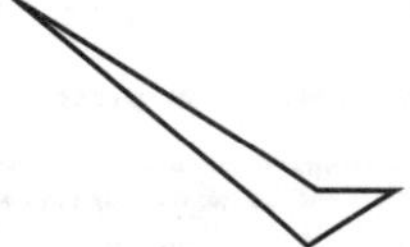

*Part I*

**Directions:** Draw the line or lines of symmetry for each shape.

1. 

2. 

3. 

4. 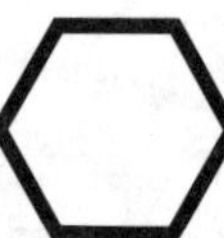

5. 

*Part II*

**Directions:** Draw six shapes of your own. Decide if each shape is symmetrical. If it is, draw the line or lines of symmetry and write the word *symmetrical.* If it is not, write the words *no symmetry.*

 

# Art and Symmetry

A figure that has *symmetry* can be folded in two so that the two parts match exactly.

**Directions:** Many artists use symmetry in their drawings and paintings. Now it's your turn to try. Look at each picture half. Draw the other half of the picture so that it is perfectly symmetrical.

When you are finished color each of your pictures, as any good artist would. Then, cut out each picture and try folding it on its line of symmetry.

1.

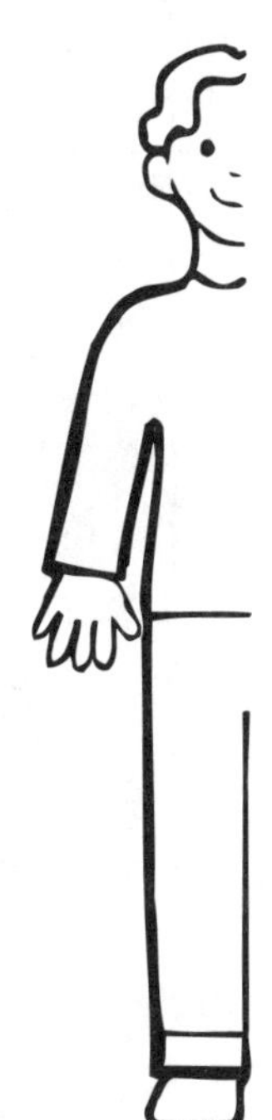

2.

3.

4.

# Tick Tock

Time is important to everyone. See how good you are at telling time by completing the exercise below.

**Directions:** Look at each clock and write the time.

# Time to Tell Time

*Part I*

**Directions:** Match each time below.

| | |
|---|---|
| 1. seven thirty | a. 9:00 |
| 2. eight fifteen | b. 7:30 |
| 3. nine o'clock | c. 12:00 |
| 4. five fifteen | d. 8:15 |
| 5. twelve noon | e. 5:15 |

*Part II*

**Directions:** Draw the time given on each empty clock face.

6.
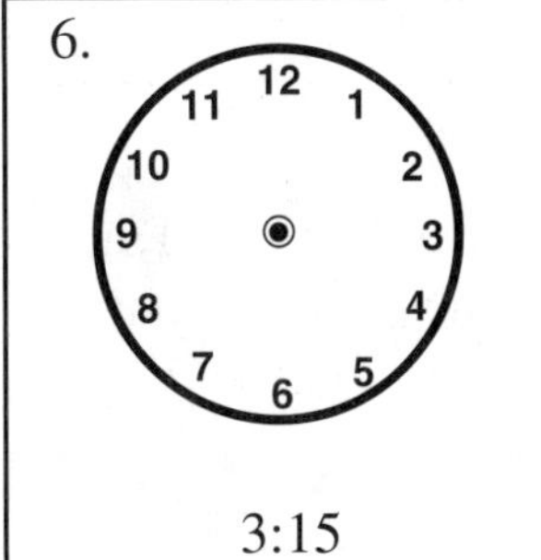
3:15

7.
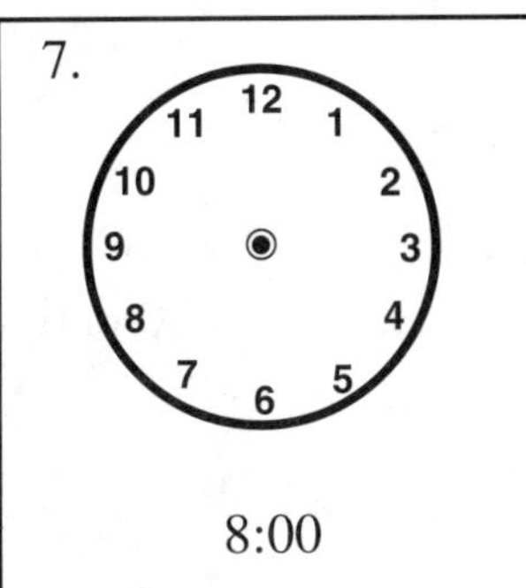
8:00

8.
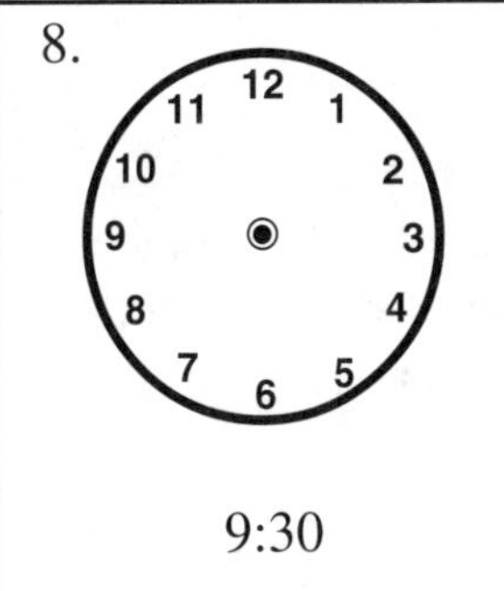
9:30

9.
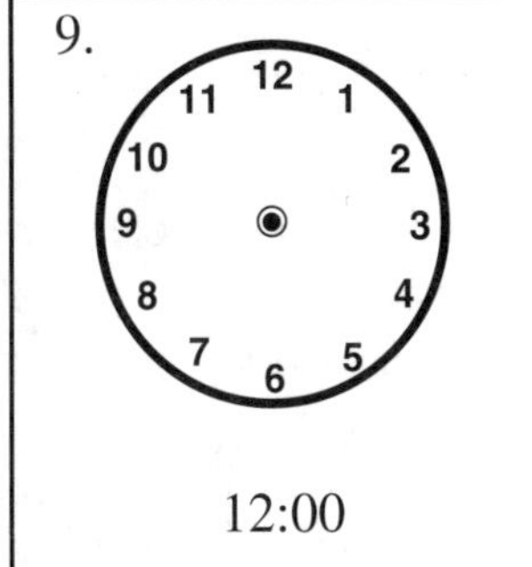
12:00

10.
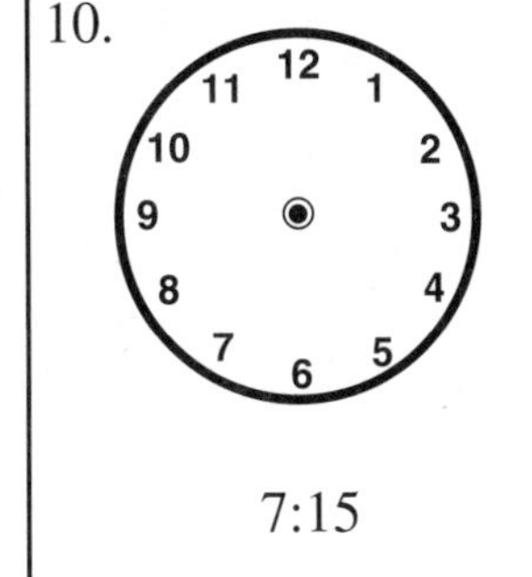
7:15

11.
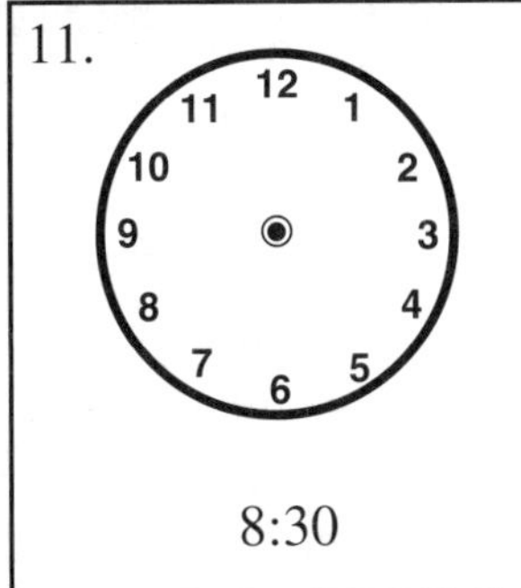
8:30

12.
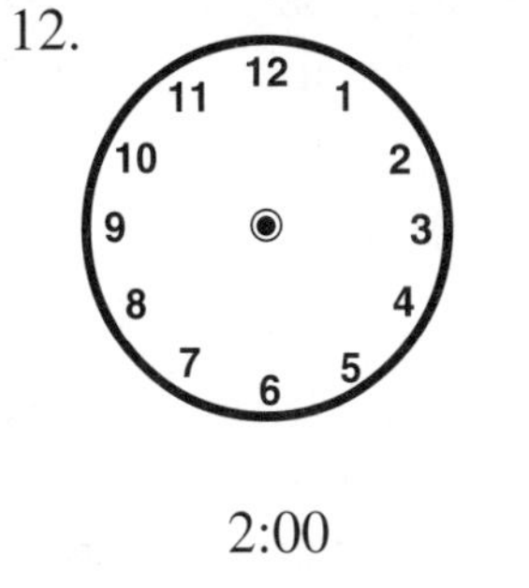
2:00

13.
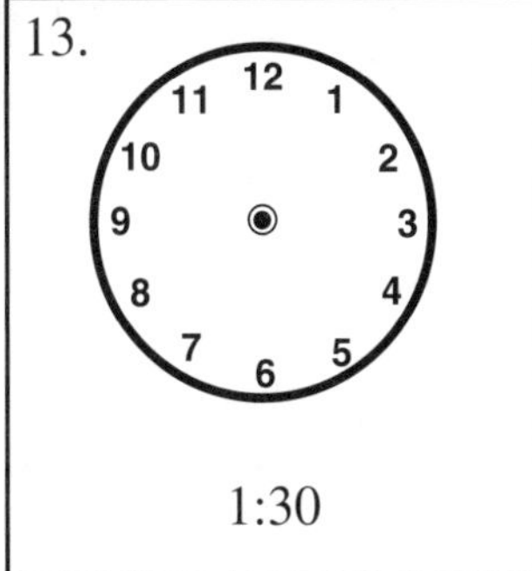
1:30

14.
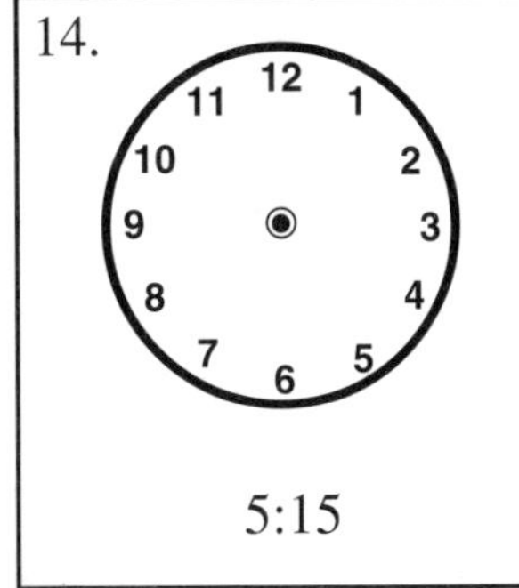
5:15

15.
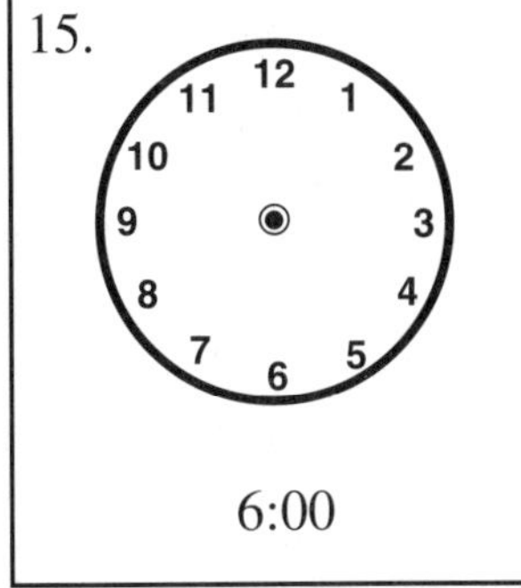
6:00

16.
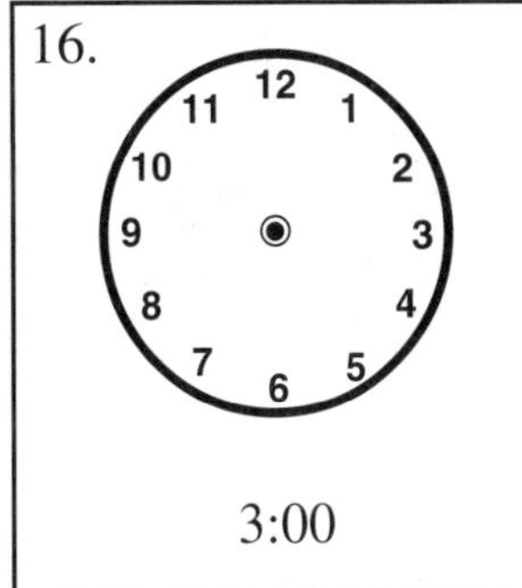
3:00

17.
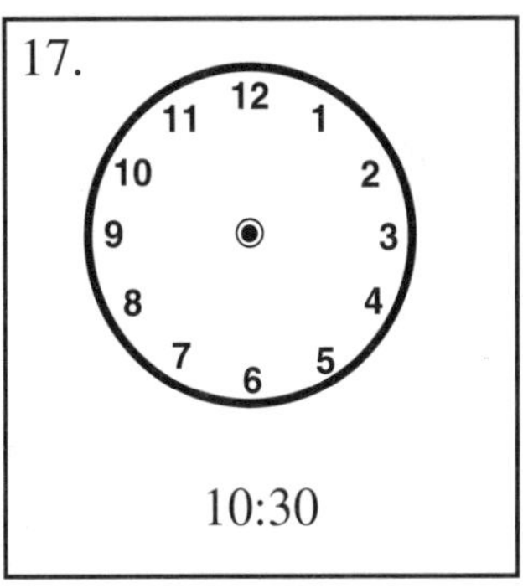
10:30

# Working with Time

**Directions:** Read and solve each word problem.

1. Margie has to be at the dentist at 6:00 o'clock. She gets off work at 4:00 o'clock. When Margie is finished with work, how much time does she have before she has to be at the dentist?

2. School starts at 7:15 in the morning. Heath's alarm goes off at 6:15 in the morning. How much time does Heath have each morning before he has to be at school?

3. Mary put her brownies in the oven at 3:00. The directions on the box said to bake the brownies for 45 minutes. At what time should Mary take the brownies out of the oven?

4. Suzy has soccer practice every Tuesday and Thursday. On Tuesday she practices from 3:00 until 4:00. However, on Thursday she has a longer practice, from 3:00 until 5:00. How many hours a week does Suzy practice soccer?

5. Brian has to be at ball practice in 30 minutes. The clock says that it is 2:15 in the afternoon. At what time should Brian arrive at the baseball park?

6. Jeanne is hungry. She and her friend Tara usually eat lunch at 11:00, but Tara is late. Jeanne decides she will wait until 1:00 for Tara, but if Tara is not ready to eat by 1:00, then Jeanne will eat without her. If Jeanne waits till 1:00 to eat, and she usually eats at 11:00, how far past her regular lunchtime will she be eating her lunch?

 

# Money! Money! Money!

Most people use money every day, so it's important to know how to count, add, and subtract money. Different countries have different systems of money. In Canada we use coins that represent many different amounts. Here are some of them:

| 1 cent | 5 cents | 10 cents | 25 cents | 50 cents |
|---|---|---|---|---|
|  | | | | |
| penny | nickel | dime | quarter | 50-cent coin |

**Directions:** Count to find each value. Write the answer on the line.

1.    = ____________

2.       = ____________

3.         = ____________

4.     = ____________

5.         = ____________

6.       = 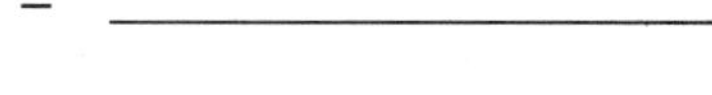

7.       = 

8.       = ____________

9.   = ____________

# Spending Your Money

**Directions:** Look at the items in the pet store window, then read and answer each question. Be sure to show your work.

1. Macey has $5.00. She wants to buy a new puppy for her birthday. She also needs to buy a dish and a bag of dog food. How much money will she need? Does she have enough money to buy everything she wants? ____________________

2. Mrs. Kramer wants to buy a pet bird. She is going to buy a parrot and a bag of birdseed. How much money will Mrs. Kramer need? ____________________

3. Olivia is going to buy a frog for her English teacher and a gerbil for her science teacher. She has $1.20. How much more money does Olivia need to buy both gifts? ____________________

4. Calvin has been saving all of his change in his piggy bank. So far, he has saved $2.68. He wants to buy his dog Roscoe a new doghouse. How much more will he need to save before he can buy the doghouse? ____________________

 

# Writing the Value

When you count money it is easiest if you start with the bill or coin that has the largest value. Of course, you should end with the bill or coin that has the smallest value.

To count this amount you should start with the 5 dollar bill, then add the 1 dollar coin, and finally add the 5 dimes. The total amount is $6.50.

**Directions:** Write each total amount.

1.     ____________

2.      ____________

3.        ____________

4.          ____________

5.   ____________

6.     ____________

7.     ____________

8.        ____________

9.   ____________

10.          ____________

# Learning About Graphs

A *graph* is a way to organize information. A *bar graph* is a graph that uses bar shapes to give information about a topic.

Look at the following graph. This graph shows how much television Michael, Jana, Kevin, and Alicia watch each day.

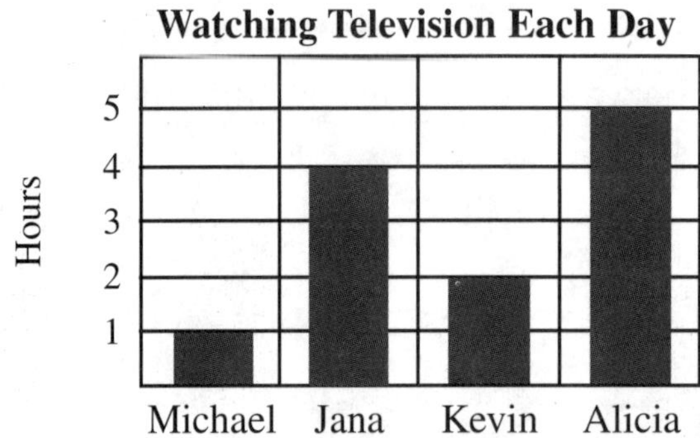


Michael watches the least television. He watches 1 hour each day.

Alicia watches the most television. She watches 5 hours each day.

What are some other things you know from looking at this graph?

*Part I*

**Directions:** Look at the bar graph and answer the questions below.

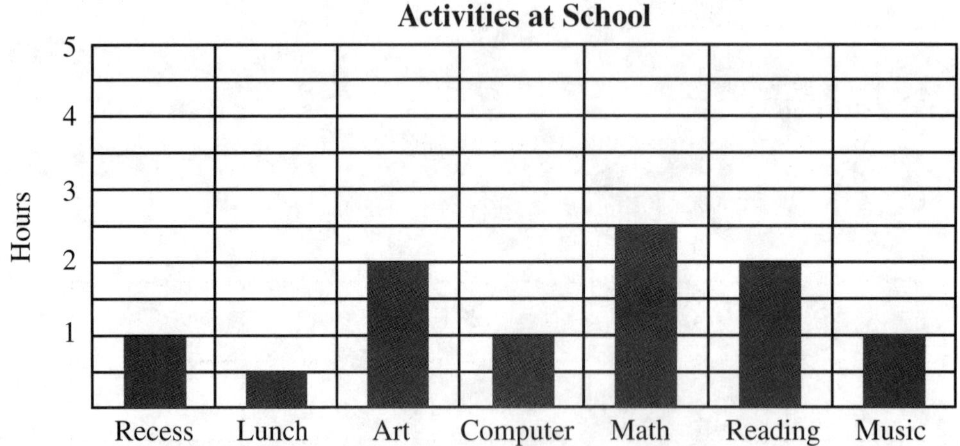


1. How many hours is math class? ______________________________

2. How long is recess? ______________________________

3. Which is longer, music class or reading class? How do you know? ______________________________

4. Which class is as long as reading class? ______________________________

5. Which class or activity is the longest? ______________________________

6. What activity or class is the shortest? ______________________________

# Graphing Your Own Day

A *bar graph* is a visual way to give information. Look at the example below.

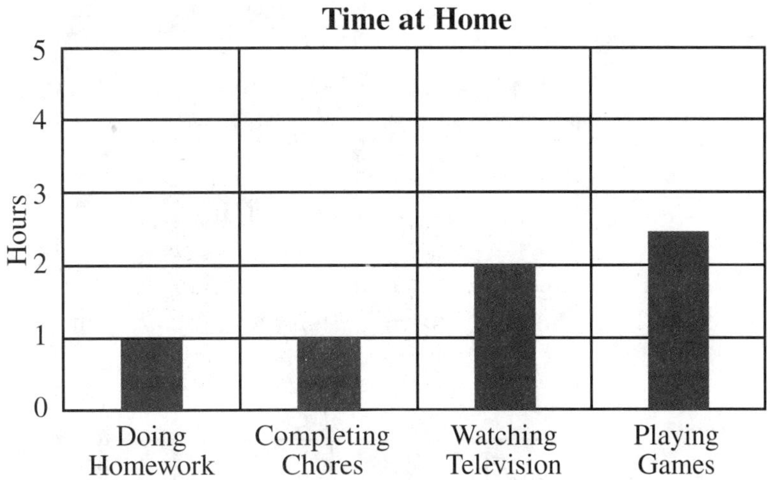


**Directions:** Make a bar graph of your own to show the information below. The outline of the graph is already drawn for you.

- Be sure to give your graph a title.
- Label the times on the left side of your graph.
- Label each activity across the bottom of your graph.
- You must list at least five activities that you do during the day.

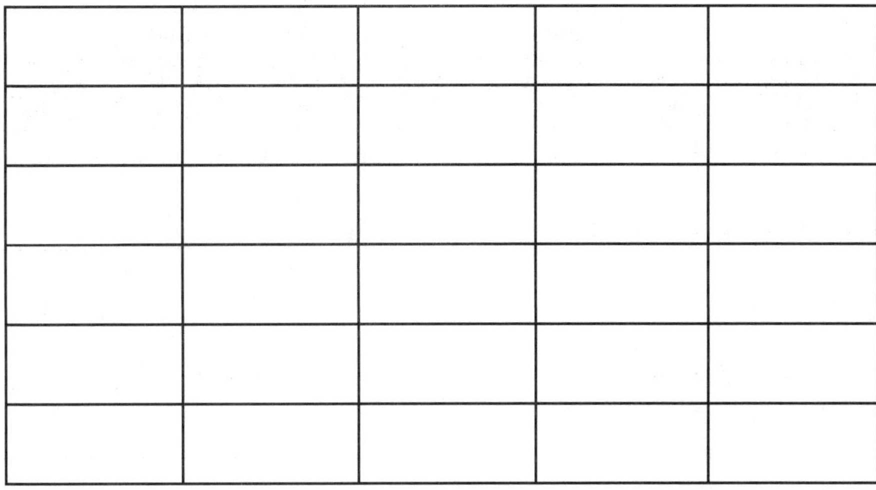

# Picture This

A *pictograph* uses pictures to represent numbers of objects. A pictograph has a *key* to show what each symbol represents. For example, if someone tried to draw a pictograph showing the number of trees in a large forest, it would take up too much paper to draw every tree. Instead, the writer would use a symbol, such as a tree, to represent a large number of trees.

1 tree symbol = 20 trees

This shows that when you see one tree, it actually represents 20 trees.

**Directions:** Tristan and his friend Ethan have been on a nature hike. As they were hiking they saw many different birds. Look at the pictograph showing what they saw on their hike and answer the questions below.

Blue Jays
Mockingbirds
Woodpeckers
Robins
Blackbirds

1 2 3 4 5 6 7

= 5 birds

1. Which bird(s) did they see the most? ____________________

2. Which bird(s) did they see the least?____________________

3. How many blue jays did they see? ____________________

4. How many total woodpeckers and blackbirds did they see?____________________

5. How many birds did they see in all? ____________________

6. Pretend they saw 20 blackbirds on their trip. Draw the symbol or symbols needed on the graph to show this many blackbirds.

 

# Vacation Spots

**Directions:** A survey was taken at Cheatham School to see where the students liked to take their vacations. The pictograph below shows how many students voted for each place. One sun represents three votes. Use the pictograph to answer the questions.

| Vacation Spots | |
|---|---|
| Toronto | |
| Myrtle Beach | |
| Gulf Shores | |
| Vancouver | |
| Cancun | |

= 3 votes

1. Which vacation spot received the most votes? ______________________

2. How many students voted for it? ______________________

3. Which two vacation spots tied? ______________________

4. How many votes did these two receive? ______________________

5. Which vacation spot received the least number of votes? ______________________

6. How many votes did it receive? ______________________

7. How many more votes did Toronto receive than Cancun? ______________________

8. According to the pictograph, how many total votes were represented? ______________________

# Tally Ho!

One way to collect numerical information is to use *tally marks*. Each slash or tally mark represents a number. If you want to show the number 3 using tally marks, then you make three slashes: / / /.

If two teams are playing a game, you can keep score using tally marks.

| The Reds | The Whites |
|---|---|
| \|\|\| | ~~\|\|\|\|~~ \|\| |

Look at the score for the second team. They have a score of 7. When you are tallying and you get to the number 5, always make a slash or tally mark that goes across the previous 4 marks, creating a group of five. Then, you start a new group of tally marks. Why? This makes your marks easier to count because you can count by fives.

**Directions:** Use tally marks to show each amount. Remember to group by 5s whenever you can.

1. The number of letters in the name of the city where you live.

2. The number of letters in your last name.

3. The number of people in your classroom. (Yes, the teacher counts as a person.)

4. The number of times you usually eat during the day.

5. The number of days in the month of December.

6. The number of people in your family.

7. The number of days in a week.

8. The number of boys in your class.

# Living Things

*Part I*

**Directions:** Read each statement. If the statement about living things is true, write True. If the statement about living things is false, write False.

________ 1. Living things never change.

________ 2. All living things must adapt to their environment.

________ 3. Living things never reproduce.

________ 4. Living things start small and usually grow larger.

________ 5. Living things rarely need light or water.

*Part II*

**Directions:** Look at the pictures below. Write the numbers 1–4 underneath each picture to place them in the correct sequence.

6. ____________________

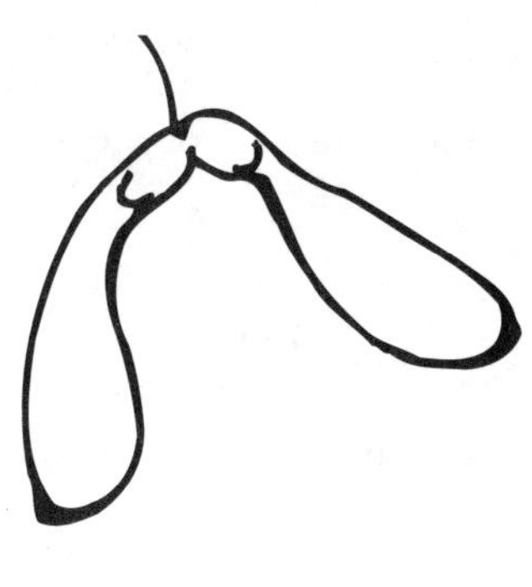

7. ____________________

8. ____________________

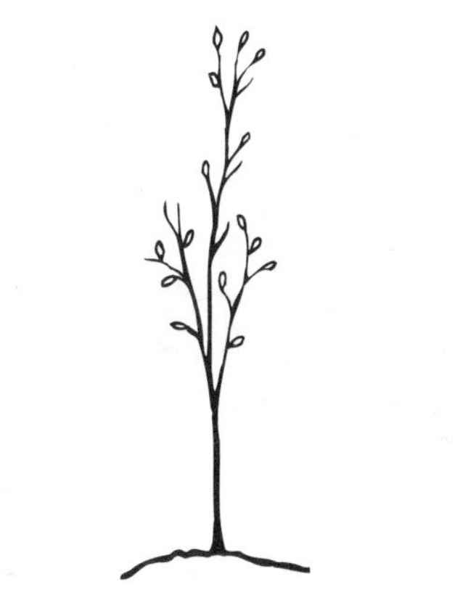

9. ____________________

# The Importance of Environment

**Directions:** All living things must adapt to their environments. Read the paragraph below and fill in the correct answers. Use the word bank to help you.

**Word Bank**

| | | | | |
|---|---|---|---|---|
| water | food | weather | desert | adapt |
| living | protection | sunlight | environment | |

A plant's or animal's ________________ is everything that is around the plant or animal. All living things must __________________________ to their environment. For example, a cactus survives the environment of the ________________ by storing water for use during long periods of time with no rain.

All living things require liquid ________________ to survive. Animals and people need energy from ________________ to grow and reproduce. ________________ is important to plants because they use it to make food in a process called photosynthesis.

________________ things are also unique because they must have protection against harsh weather conditions. When the ________________ gets bad, living things must be ready. People must find ________________ during storms. One way to do this is to seek shelter. Plants must also have protection against the weather. Trees and plants are often able to bend with a strong wind rather than break during bad weather.

 

# Parts of a Plant

*Part I*

**Directions:** Color the picture below. Then, use the word bank to label the parts of the plant.

| Word Bank | | | |
|---|---|---|---|
| flower | leaf | stem | roots |

*Part II*

**Directions:** Answer each question.

1. Which part of the plant has the seeds? ____________________
2. Which part of the plant helps keep the plant straight and upright? ____________________
3. Which part of the plant helps the plant get water from the ground? ____________________
4. Which part of the plant that is above ground helps make food for the plant? ____________________
5. Which part of the plant is attractive to some insects? ____________________
6. Which part of the plant takes in minerals from the soil? ____________________

# Parts with Purpose

**Directions:** Write the number of the correct description next to each picture.

1. 

2. ________

3. ________

4. ________

5. ________

6. ________

7. ________

8. ________

9. ________

10. ________

a. This animal's feathers, called down, help keep it warm.

b. This animal's long tail keeps insects away from its body.

c. This animal's fur blends in with its wooded environment.

d. This animal's speed helps it escape from would-be predators.

e. This animal's ability to camouflage itself makes it practically invisible in its environment.

f. This animal's sharp teeth are used for protection and to attack.

g. This animal's sharp claws are used to hunt prey at night.

h. This animal's ability to climb helps it find safety and food.

i. This animal's sharp quills keep predators away.

j. This animal's strong legs help it jump and attack.

# Life Cycles

Animals change as they grow, but all animals do not change and grow in the same way. One example of this is the butterfly. The butterfly starts as an egg. From the egg, a caterpillar is born. Eventually the caterpillar forms a casing around itself and becomes a pupa. After about a week, a beautiful butterfly emerges from the pupa.

**Directions:** Think for a minute about your own life cycle. Draw at least five pictures showing the stages of life you have experienced and/or will experience. Beside each picture, write at least one characteristic that is unique to each stage of development.

| Life Stage | Unique Characteristic |
| --- | --- |
| | |
| | |
| | |
| | |
| | |

# Heredity or Not?

Heredity deals with the characteristics an organism inherits from its parents. For example, if you have blue eyes and your parents have blue eyes, this is a trait you have inherited. Some characteristics are not inherited but are learned traits. A person's manners are an example of a learned trait.

*Part I*

**Directions:** Read each example. If it is an inherited trait, write the letter *I*. If it is a learned trait, write the letter *L*.

________ 1. Big feet

________ 2. Being able to swim

________ 3. Naturally curly hair

________ 4. A good singing voice

________ 5. Being able to name all the provinces

________ 6. Being short or tall

________ 7. A positive attitude

________ 8. Freckles

________ 9. Getting good grades in school

________10. Being polite

*Part II*

**Directions:** On the back of this page, draw a picture of yourself. Then list at least four traits about you that are inherited traits rather than learned traits.

1. ________________________________________

2. ________________________________________

3. ________________________________________

4. ________________________________________

 

# Not Your Typical Grocery Store

For plants and animals, the world outside is like a grocery store; it's a giant source of food. Some animals eat only plants. These animals are herbivores. Some animals eat only meat. These animals are carnivores. Some animals eat both plants and meat. These animals are omnivores.

**Directions:** Inside each cart, write h(*herbivore),* c(*carnivore),* or o(*omnivore)* to describe each animal.

# Food Chains and Food Webs

All living things need food to get energy. Some living things can make their own food. They are called *producers*. A *consumer* is a living thing that cannot make its own food. Some consumers, called *herbivores*, eat only plants. Other consumers, called *carnivores*, eat only meat. Still others are known as *omnivores* because they eat both plants and meat. There are some living things that break down and consume dead plants and animals. These organisms are called *decomposers*. All of these living and nonliving things create what is known as a *food chain*. A food chain explains how a living thing gets the food it needs for energy. When a food chain links to another food chain, it becomes a *food web*.

**Directions:** Draw a line to match each statement to its ending.

| | |
|---|---|
| 1. Organisms that can make their own food are called | a. ecosystem |
| 2. In a food chain, organisms transfer | b. carnivores |
| 3. Food chains that link to other food chains become a | c. food |
| 4. Animals that eat only plants are called | d. decomposers |
| 5. Animals that eat only other animals are called | e. energy |
| 6. A consumer is an organism that does not make its own | f. producers |
| 7. Organisms that break down dead plants and animals are called | g. herbivores |
| 8. All living and nonliving things in an area make up an | h. food web |

**Something extra:** List four animals that are herbivores and four animals that are carnivores.

| Herbivores | Carnivores |
|---|---|
| ______________________ | ______________________ |
| ______________________ | ______________________ |
| ______________________ | ______________________ |
| ______________________ | ______________________ |

Can you think of any animals that are omnivores?

______________________________________________

______________________________________________

 

# The World Around You

All living organisms need energy. Living things get energy from the food they eat. An animal that eats only plants for its energy is called an herbivore, an animal that eats only meat for its energy is called a carnivore, and an animal that eats both plants and meat for its energy is called an omnivore. Animals live in habitats where their energy needs can be met.

A food chain shows how living organisms are connected. For example, in a food chain grass would be eaten by a rabbit, and then the rabbit would be eaten by a fox. Each part of the chain is needed to supply energy to the next living organism. Organisms called decomposers break down any leftover food, the nutrients enter the soil to feed plants, and the cycle starts all over again.

**Directions:** Read each question, and then circle the correct answer.

1. All living organisms need

   a. grass b. energy

2. Nutrients are recycled back to the earth by

   a. decomposers b. photosynthesis

3. An organism's home might also be called its

   a. life cycle b. habitat

4. An animal that eats only plants is called

   a. hungry b. an herbivore

5. An animal that eats only meat is called

   a. a carnivore b. an omnivore

6. An organism that eats both plants and animals is called

   a. an omnivore b. a producer

7. In the food chain a lion would most likely eat

   a. plants b. animals

8. A food chain shows how living organisms are

   a. connected b. decompose

# Pyramids...Not Just for Egypt

**Directions:** Energy pyramids are diagrams that show how energy moves through an ecosystem.

**Example:**

Look at the energy pyramids below and decide what might go in each missing section. Draw a picture and write the name of the plant or animal.

1. 2. 3. 4.

5. 6. 7.

# You and Your Food

Just as other organisms get their energy from a food chain or web, so do humans.

**Directions:** Think about your eating habits. Write down everything you ate for breakfast, lunch, dinner, and any snacks. Then answer the questions below.

Breakfast: ____________________

____________________

____________________

Lunch: ____________________

____________________

____________________

Dinner: ____________________

____________________

____________________

Snacks: ____________________

____________________

____________________

1. Look over your menu. Are your eating habits more like a herbivore, carnivore, or an omnivore?

____________________

____________________

____________________

2. Choose one item from your menu and create an energy pyramid with you at the top of the pyramid.

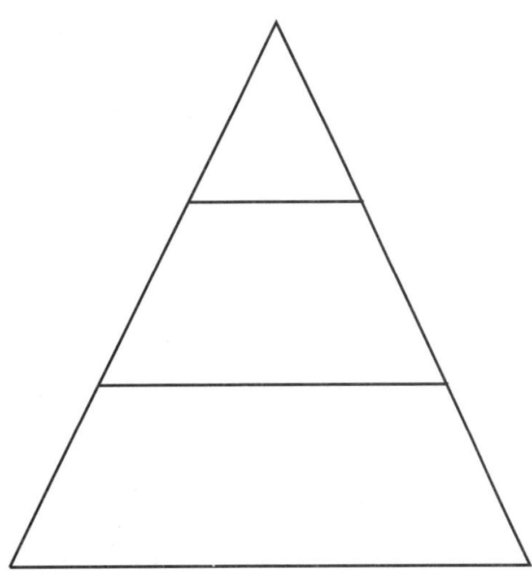

# We're All in This Together

Humans make many positive and negative changes affecting the Earth and its ecosystems.

**Directions:** Color the picture of our world. Then, list five ways people can cause negative changes to the world's ecosystems and five ways people can cause positive changes to the world's ecosystems.

Negative changes:

1. ______________________________

______________________________

______________________________

2. ______________________________

______________________________

______________________________

______________________________

3. ______________________________

______________________________

______________________________

4. ______________________________

______________________________

______________________________

5. ______________________________

______________________________

______________________________

Positive changes:

1. ______________________________

______________________________

______________________________

2. ______________________________

______________________________

______________________________

______________________________

3. ______________________________

______________________________

______________________________

4. ______________________________

______________________________

______________________________

5. ______________________________

______________________________

______________________________

 

# Rocks and Minerals

Not everything on Earth is a plant or an animal. The Earth is also made up of many other things including *minerals* and *rocks*. Minerals are nonliving substances occurring in nature. Minerals combine with each other to make up rocks.

There are three main types of rocks: igneous, sedimentary, and metamorphic. Igneous rocks are formed when hot, molten rock cools and then becomes a solid. Sedimentary rock is formed from sand, mud, or pebbles that pile up on the bottom of rivers, lakes, etc. Metamorphic rocks are formed when existing igneous or sedimentary rock is changed because of heat or pressure from the Earth.

**Directions:** Color only the rocks that have statements that are true. Place an X on the rocks that have statements that are false.

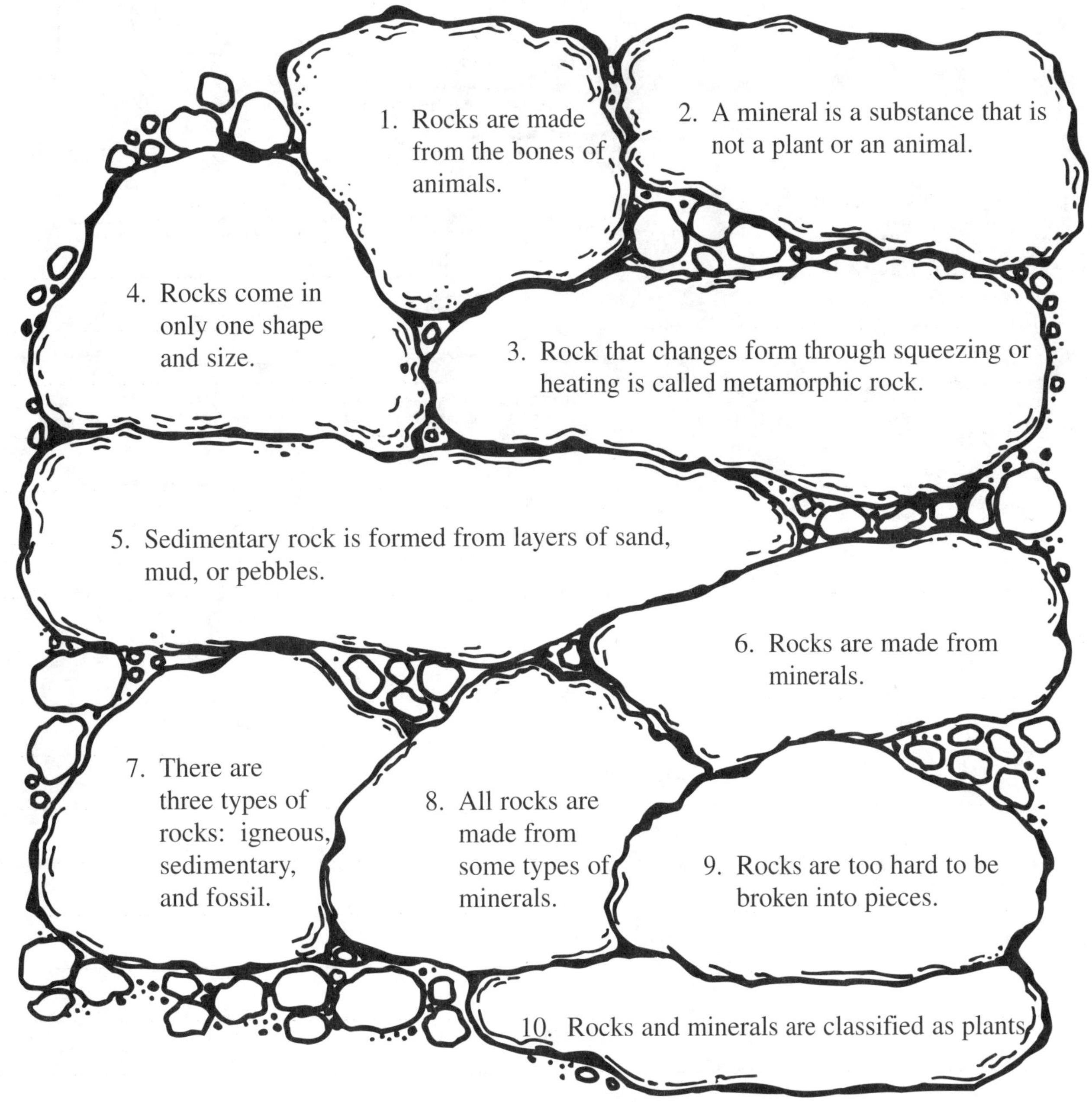

# Here's the Dirt

**Directions:** Look at the picture below. Draw at least five things that can grow in the soil. Be sure to color your picture when you are finished.

List at least 3 things your plants would need to help them grow.

1. ______________________________

2. ______________________________

3. ______________________________

 

# Long, Long Ago

The imprint or remains of something in the earth that lived long, long ago is called a fossil.

*Part I*

**Directions:** Draw a line and match each fossil to what formed it.

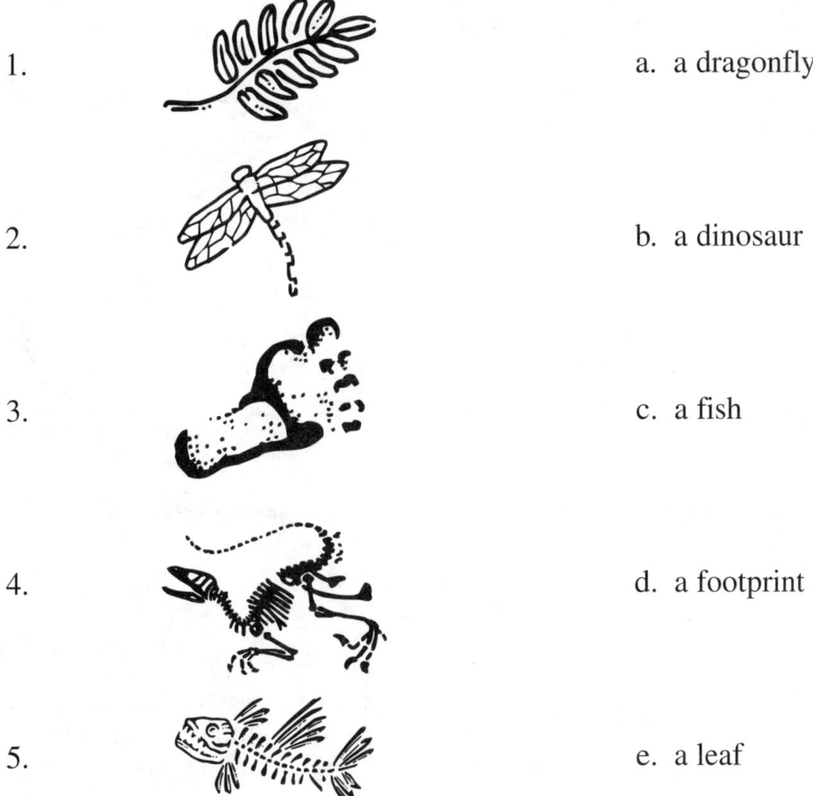

1. a. a dragonfly

2. b. a dinosaur

3. c. a fish

4. d. a footprint

5. e. a leaf

*Part II*

**Directions:** Color the fossils you find.

# Finding Out More About Fossils

Fossils are imprints found on the Earth that tell about things from the past. Because they are discoveries from the past, scientists use fossils today to study how the world has changed. Today's fossil scientists, called paleontologists, are always discovering something new about the world by studying fossils. Fossils are unique not only because they give information about the past but also because they are found in so many shapes, sizes, and places. Some fossils have even been found in the hardened amber that comes from trees. Still other fossils are found in the layers of the Earth's rocks and soil. Fossils are indeed a map to the past.

**Directions:** Color the fossils that have statements that are true.

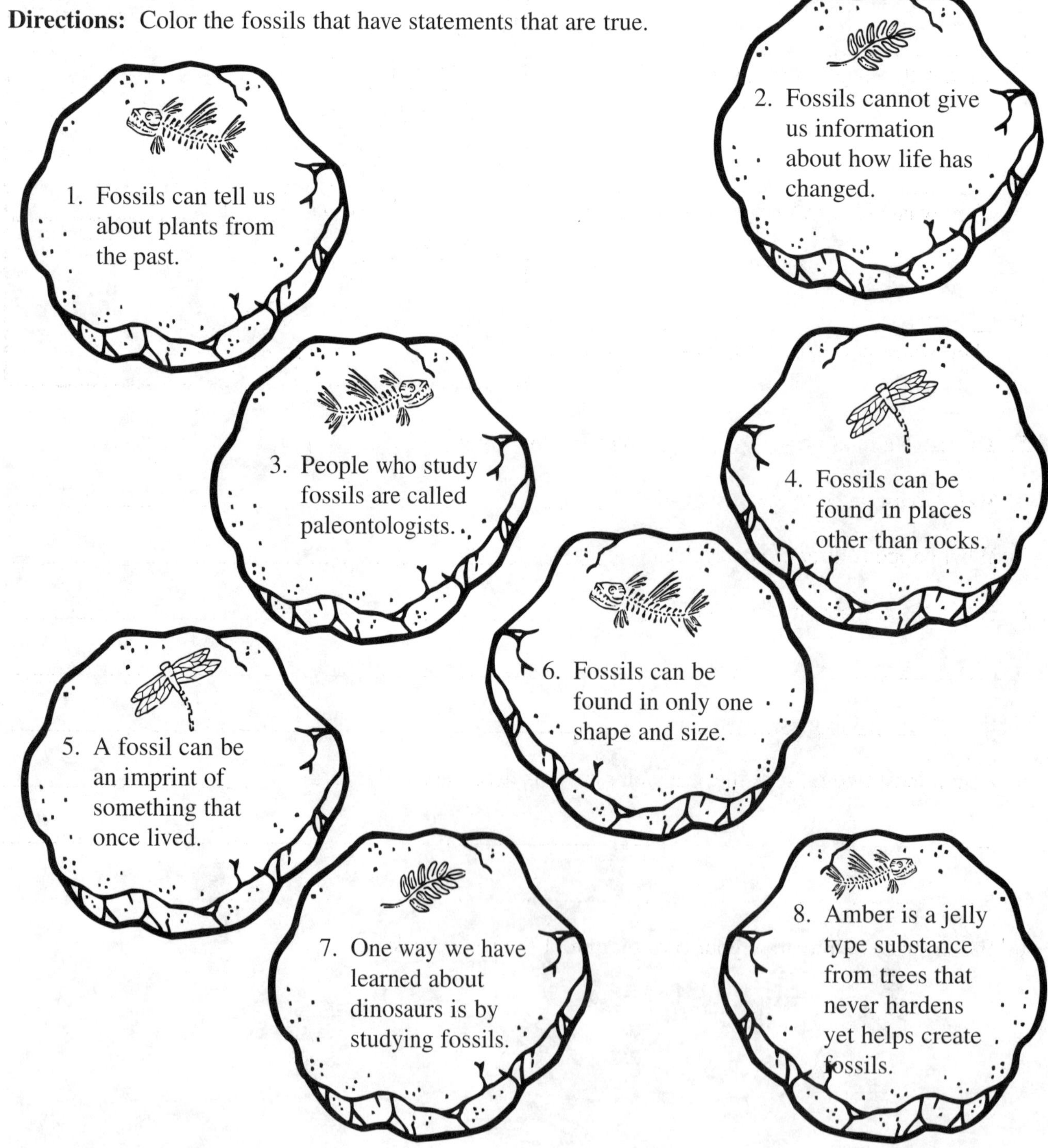

# Water, Water Everywhere!

**Directions:** We all know that we need water to survive. Water on Earth moves in a continuous cycle from the Earth to the sky and back again. Look at the diagram below, and then fill in the blanks.

condensation
precipitation
evaporation
runoff

1. ______________________________ is when water changes from liquid to vapor.

2. ______________________________ is when water vapor changes to liquid.

3. ______________________________ is when water falls from clouds to the Earth.

4. ______________________________ is when water pools in lakes, seas, and oceans.

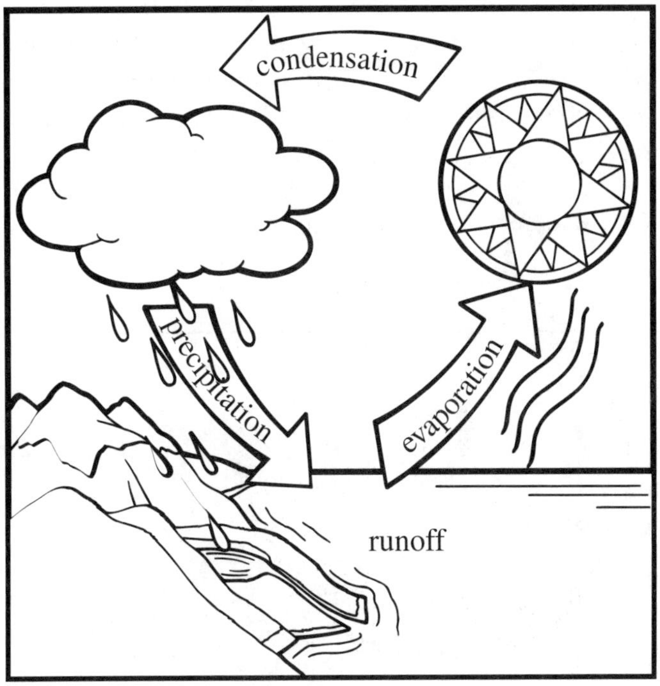

5. There are a total of __________ steps in the water cycle.

6. Water that rises into the air is called ______________________________

7. What happens after condensation? ______________________________

8. Name three types of precipitation.______________________________

______________________________

______________________________

9. List at least two reasons that the water cycle is necessary to the earth. ____________

______________________________

______________________________

10. In the space below draw your own picture of the water cycle.

# Find that Hidden Word

**Directions:** Search across, down, and diagonally to find the words hidden in the word search. Use the word bank to help you in your search.

**Word Bank**

| | | | |
|---|---|---|---|
| condensation | precipitation | evaporation | sun |
| rain | sleet | snow | rivers |
| oceans | water | lakes | temperature |

| | | | | | | | | | | | | | | |
|---|---|---|---|---|---|---|---|---|---|---|---|---|---|---|
| T | N | F | P | S | E | R | T | T | Y | R | S | N | G | E |
| E | U | E | U | E | I | E | R | E | V | O | O | V | B | A |
| M | Y | N | W | V | V | T | M | I | E | I | P | M | H | E |
| P | F | M | E | U | Z | A | Q | U | T | L | D | G | L | F |
| E | E | R | T | D | H | W | P | A | A | Q | S | C | S | S |
| R | S | H | B | L | R | R | T | O | L | Y | Y | L | N | R |
| A | R | Q | L | R | D | I | M | O | R | C | K | Q | O | A |
| T | A | Y | J | T | P | H | N | C | N | A | H | R | W | K |
| U | Q | C | U | I | K | T | R | V | R | F | T | Q | C | J |
| R | R | W | C | P | L | A | K | E | S | Y | V | I | Y | Z |
| E | Z | E | C | O | N | D | E | N | S | A | T | I | O | N |
| I | R | U | S | I | Q | A | R | S | N | A | E | C | O | N |
| P | R | P | R | O | Q | K | M | A | Q | C | I | E | Q | C |
| G | S | E | J | C | I | A | T | L | I | C | U | U | S | L |
| M | Q | N | K | Q | E | E | W | I | L | N | P | W | Q | J |

# Night and Day

*Part I*

**Directions:** Answer each question below.

List three things you normally do when it is daylight.

1. ______________________________

2. ______________________________

3. ______________________________

List three things you normally do when it is dark.

4. ______________________________

5. ______________________________

6. ______________________________

*Part II*

**Directions:** Read the short paragraph and then answer the questions.

Night and day are caused by the Earth's rotation on its axis. Where the Earth is turned away from the sun, it is night. Where the Earth is turned towards the sun, it is day. It takes 24 hours for the Earth to make a complete rotation. This 24-hour rotation makes one day.

7. How long does it take for the earth to make a complete rotation? ______________

8. What causes the Earth to have night and day? ______________________________

______________________________

9. When it is day, part of the Earth is turned towards the ______________.

10. When it is night, part of the Earth is turned ______________ from the sun.

# The Sun and the Moon

You know that night and day are caused by the Earth's rotation on its axis. As the Earth turns, the part of the Earth facing the sun has day. The part of the Earth not facing the sun has night. Because of the sun and the moon and the rotation of the Earth, we have light and dark or day and night. This rotation of the Earth helps you decide when to do many of your daily activities.

**Directions:** Look at each picture below. If the event usually occurs in the day, draw a sun next to the picture. If the event usually occurs at night, draw a moon next to the picture.

1. 

2. 

3. 

4. 

5. 

6. 

# Best Choice

**Directions:** Read the information and then read each question. Circle the answer that is the best choice.

Our planet Earth is part of a solar system that is made up of the sun and all the objects that orbit the sun. The planets that are in our solar system are commonly divided into two groups. These groups are known as the inner planets and the outer planets. The inner planets are the planets that are closest to the sun. The outer planets are the planets that are not as close to the sun. Earth is considered an inner planet. The Earth rotates or spins on its axis. It takes the Earth 24 hours, or one day, to complete a rotation.

The moon is also part of our solar system. The moon goes through different phases depending on the amount of light it gets from the sun. Although the shape of the moon does not really change, the moon appears to change in shape as it goes through its four phases.

1. Earth makes a complete rotation in…

   a. 24 hours.

   b. 1 week.

2. The solar system is made up of the sun and all of the objects that…

   a. orbit the sun.

   b. are in outer space.

3. Earth rotates or spins on its…

   a. northern side.

   b. axis.

4. The moon goes through…

   a. two phases.

   b. four phases.

5. The planets are divided into two groups: the inner planets and…

   a. the outer planets .

   b. the larger planets.

# The Man in the Moon

Just as the Earth orbits the sun, the moon orbits the Earth. Because of this orbit, the moon appears to change shapes. The apparent changes of the moon are called its phases. As you gaze at the moon you may even see what looks like a face, otherwise known as the Man in the Moon. The face is, in fact, nothing more than craters on the moon's surface.

*Part I*

**Directions:** Look at the pictures of the moon. Use the word bank to help you label the different phases of the moon.

| **Word Bank** | | | |
|---|---|---|---|
| Last quarter moon | First quarter moon | New moon | Full moon |

______________ ______________ ______________ ______________

*Part II*

**Directions:** Imagine that there really is a man in the moon. Write a short explanation telling who he is and how he got there. Explain why he stays on the moon. Then, on the back of this sheet, draw your own picture of the man in the moon.

________________________________________

________________________________________

________________________________________

________________________________________

________________________________________

________________________________________

________________________________________

________________________________________

# What's Out There?

*Part I*

**Directions:** Label and color each planet/dwarf planet in our solar system. Use the word bank if you need help.

| Word Bank | | | | | | | | |
|---|---|---|---|---|---|---|---|---|
| Mercury | Venus | Earth | Mars | Jupiter | Saturn | Uranus | Neptune | Pluto |

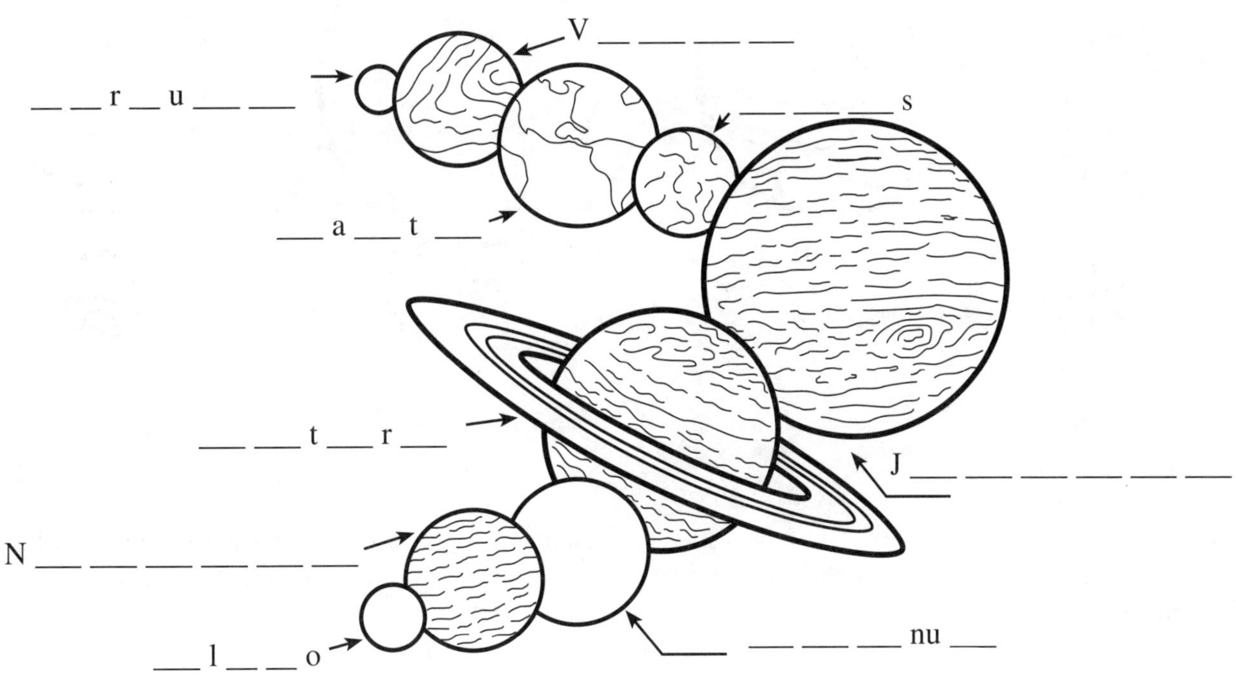


*Part II*

**Directions:** If you could create a new planet for our solar system, what would you name it? What would it look like? Where would you place it among the planets? Would your planet have anyone living on it?

Write about your new planet, and then draw a picture of your new planet. Use your own piece of paper or the back of this one if you need more space.

______________________________________________

______________________________________________

______________________________________________

______________________________________________

______________________________________________

______________________________________________

# The Inner Planets

*Part I*

**Directions:** Below are the four inner planets drawn left to right in order from the sun. Color each planet.

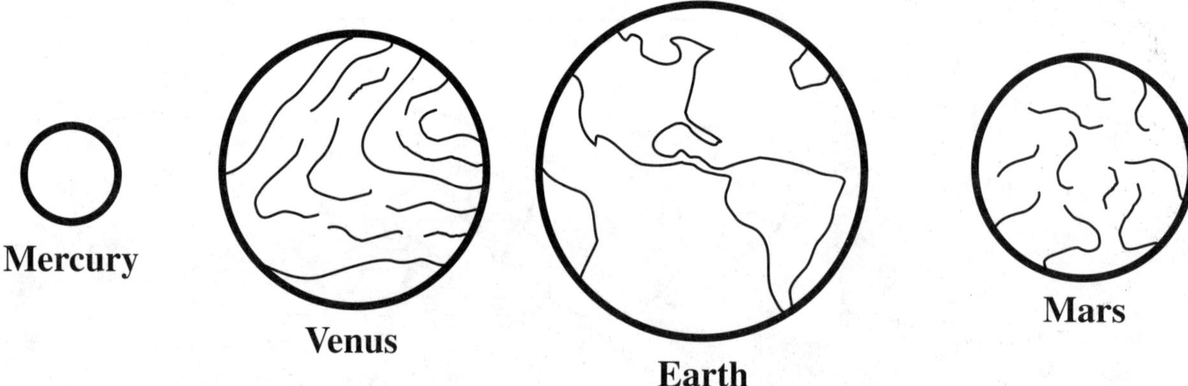


*Part II*

**Directions:** Answer each question about the four inner planets.

1. ________________________ is one of the inner planets, and it is closest to the sun.
2. ________________________ is the inner planet that was named after a female goddess. It is the second-closest planet to the sun.
3. Our planet, ________________________ , is also one of the inner planets. It is sometimes called "the third rock from the sun".
4. The inner planet known as "the Red Planet" is ________________________ . It is the last of the inner planets.
5. Planet Earth gets its light from the ________________________ .
6. On which inner planet do you live? ________________________

 

# The Outer Planets

*Part I*

**Directions:** Below are the five outer planets drawn in order left to right from the sun and the inner planets. Color each planet. (Note: Pluto has recently been reclassified as a dwarf planet.)

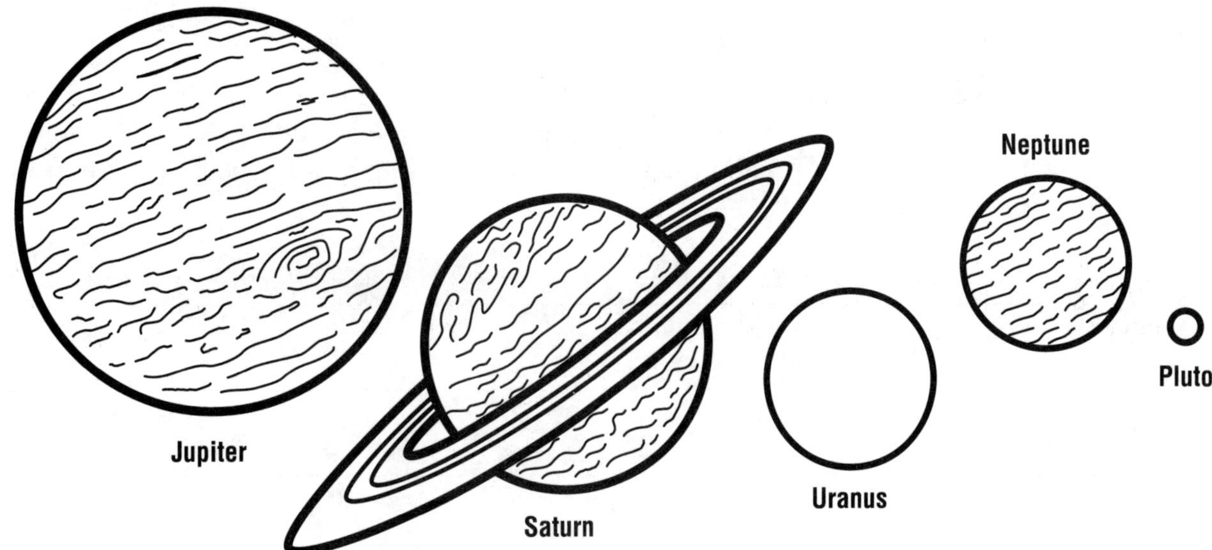


*Part II*

**Directions:** Use the pictures above to help you match each planet to its correct answer.

| | |
|---|---|
| 1. Neptune | a. This planet is the third of the outer planets. |
| 2. Jupiter | b. Farthest from the sun, this is now known as a dwarf planet. |
| 3. Saturn | c. This planet is the largest planet in our solar system. |
| 4. Pluto | d. This planet is known for the rings that circle it. |
| 5. Uranus | e. This planet is the fourth outer planet and was named after the god of the sea in Roman mythology. |

# Gravity – the Force That's Really with You

Gravity is an invisible force that pulls objects towards the Earth. The further away an object is the less gravity acts as a force on the object. For example, the moon is held in orbit by Earth's gravitational pull but because the moon is so far away, gravity does not pull the moon into the Earth. However, if you went outside and picked up a ball and then dropped it, the ball would immediately fall to the ground. This is an example of gravity in action.

**Directions:** Imagine you wake up one morning and you and everything in your bedroom are floating off the ground. For one day only there is no gravity on the Earth. How would your day be different? What would be harder to do? What would be easier to do? Write a short story about your day without gravity.

# Going to the Races

Motion and speed are terms we use when talking about how an object moves.

*Motion:* An object is in motion if it is changing position.

*Speed:* Speed is a measure of an object's rate of motion. Speed is usually measured by the time it takes for an object to travel a certain distance. If an object moves faster, its speed increases. If an object slows down, its speed decreases.

**Directions:** Read the statement on each car about motion and speed. If the statement is a fact, color the race car. If the statement is not a fact, do nothing to the race car.

# Push and Pull

Pushes and pulls are forces. A force is able to change the motion of an object. Of course, the heavier an object is the more force it takes to move that object.

**Directions:** Look at each picture. Write "push" if you would push the object to move it. Write "pull" if you would pull the object to move it.

1. RED ______________
2. ______________
3. ______________
4. ______________
5. ______________
6. ______________
7. ______________
8. ______________
9. ______________
10. ______________
11. ______________
12. ______________

**Something Extra:** Try to think of something you both push and pull. For example, you both push and pull a vacuum cleaner. See how many objects you can list.

______________________________

______________________________

______________________________

______________________________

______________________________

______________________________

______________________________

______________________________

 

# Green Light, Red Light

Motion can be seen when a car approaches a stoplight. If the light is green, the driver pushes the gas pedal and the force of the engine keeps the car moving. Force can change the direction and speed of an object, like when a bat hits a baseball.

If the light turns red, the driver pushes the brakes, which use friction to slow the car down. Friction is produced when two materials rub against each other and causes an object in motion to slow down or stop. Friction can also cause heat—try rubbing your hands together quickly. Can you feel the heat caused by friction?

**Directions:** Circle the best answer.

1. ___________ happens when an object rubs against another object.

    a. friction

    b. motion

2. Friction can cause an object to _____________

    a. move faster

    b. slow down or stop

3. A ________________ can change the motion of an object.

    a. distance

    b. force

4. A force can cause an object in motion to ________________

    a. speed up

    b. be heavier

5. Friction can create ________________

    a. distance

    b. heat

# Magnetic Attraction

A magnet is a special object that can attract certain metals like iron or steel. This magnetic attraction or pull is called magnetic force. Some metals like copper or aluminum are not attracted to magnets; there would be no push or pull if a magnet was placed near one of these metals. Magnets have both positive and negative poles. These poles can cause magnets to push or pull another magnet.

*Part I*

**Directions:** Look at each object below. If the object could be attracted to a magnet, circle it. If there would be no attraction or motion, place an X on the object.

# Crossword Fun

**Directions:** Complete the crossword puzzle by answering each question.

| Word Bank | |
|---|---|
| motion | push |
| stopped | forces |
| gravity | position |
| pull | speed |

**Across**

3. If an object changes its ________________, then it is in motion.
5. Pushes and pulls are examples of ____________.
6. An example of a force used to move a toy wagon would be a ____________.
7. How fast or slow an object is moving is the object's ____________.

**Down**

1. Things fall to Earth because of ____________.
2. Force is what puts an object in ____________.
3. An example of a force used to move a baby stroller would be a ____________.
4. When an object is no longer in motion, the object has ____________.

# Name that Substance

A *solid* has definite shape, mass, and volume. An example is an apple you can eat.

A *liquid* has no definite shape, but it does have mass and volume. An example is orange juice you can drink.

A *gas* has no definite shape, mass, or volume. An example is steam from a boiling pot.

**Directions:** Label each substance as a solid, liquid, or gas.

| Substance | Form |
|---|---|
| 1. water | ________________ |
| 2. oxygen | ________________ |
| 3. wood | ________________ |
| 4. juice | ________________ |
| 5. helium | ________________ |
| 6. concrete | ________________ |
| 7. ice | ________________ |
| 8. lemonade | ________________ |
| 9. nitrogen | ________________ |
| 10. milk | ________________ |
| 11. tea | ________________ |
| 12. metal | ________________ |
| 13. coffee | ________________ |
| 14. hydrogen | ________________ |
| 15. steel | ________________ |

 

# Solid, Liquid, and Gas

*Part I*

Matter can be classified as a solid, a liquid, or a gas. List five examples of each of the different states of matter.

| | Solid | Liquid | Gas |
|---|---|---|---|
| **Example:** | wood | water | hydrogen |
| | 1. ________ | 1. ________ | 1. ________ |
| | 2. ________ | 2. ________ | 2. ________ |
| | 3. ________ | 3. ________ | 3. ________ |
| | 4. ________ | 4. ________ | 4. ________ |
| | 5. ________ | 5. ________ | 5. ________ |

*Part II*

**Directions:** In the space below draw and label examples of matter in the state of a solid and matter in the state of a liquid. Do not use any of the examples you listed above.

| Solid | Liquid |
|---|---|
| | |

# More or Less

Mass is the amount of matter in an object. Matter is made up of particles. When the particles are tightly packed the object has more mass. Therefore, the more mass an object has, the more the object will weigh.

**Directions:** Circle the object that has more mass.

1.

2.

3.

4.

5.

6.

7.

8.

9.

10.

11.

12.

13.

14.

15.

16.

17.

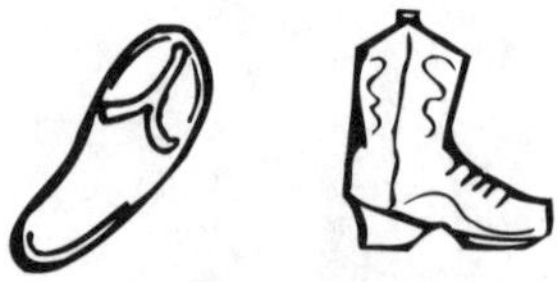

18.

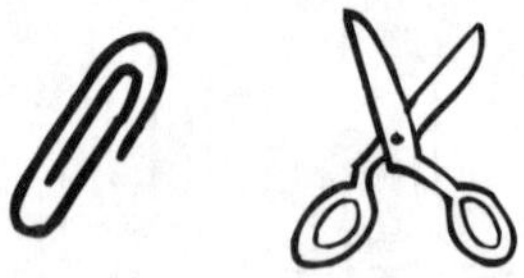

19.

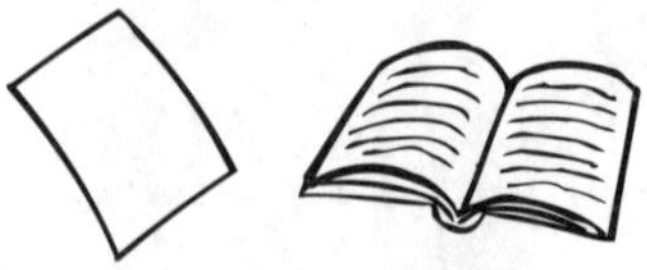

20.

# What's the Matter?

**Directions:** Answer each question below. Use the word bank if you need help.

| Word Bank | | | | |
|---|---|---|---|---|
| properties | mass | size | color | gas |
| particles | weight | solid | liquid | shape |

1. Matter can be described by its characteristics or ________________ .
2. Three characteristics of matter are ______________ , ______________, and ______________.
3. Oxygen is an example of matter that is a ________________.
4. Water is an example of matter that is a ________________.
5. Ice is an example of matter that is a ________________.
6. ________________ is the amount of matter in an object.
7. The more mass an object has, the more ________________ an object has on Earth.
8. Matter is made up of ___________; the more tightly packed they are, the more an object weighs.

# Find That Word!

**Directions:** Find the words hidden in the word search. Words can be hidden horizontally, vertically, or diagonally.

| | | | | | | | | | | | | | | |
|---|---|---|---|---|---|---|---|---|---|---|---|---|---|---|
| M | V | T | S | U | G | W | F | W | Z | J | S | S | H | S |
| K | A | H | E | Y | R | E | T | A | W | O | E | I | N | Z |
| T | F | T | I | W | O | I | M | A | L | L | E | P | C | X |
| Y | O | K | T | Z | E | G | Q | I | C | M | G | A | S | E |
| F | P | Q | R | E | U | H | D | I | K | N | A | Q | T | X |
| B | B | H | E | U | R | T | T | B | J | U | D | E | K | H |
| M | J | R | P | N | N | R | S | C | D | P | M | Z | T | N |
| N | P | I | O | U | A | F | S | J | R | B | T | Y | Q | S |
| I | T | U | R | P | Y | D | A | C | M | W | R | Y | Y | Q |
| X | V | W | P | L | F | F | M | F | I | B | C | M | E | S |
| F | B | K | V | R | L | G | Q | M | S | N | R | U | J | H |
| L | I | Q | U | I | D | I | C | T | L | O | A | B | J | N |
| F | G | V | E | J | T | T | K | Y | F | F | U | E | A | E |
| Q | S | P | B | I | S | P | U | N | L | R | S | I | Q | S |
| Y | U | B | E | Q | Q | S | W | X | B | C | B | O | V | W |

| | | | |
|---|---|---|---|
| solid | matter | weight | ice |
| gas | properties | particles | steam |
| liquid | mass | water | form |

 

# Answer Key

**Page 30**

Answers will vary

**Page 31**

1. C
3. C
4. C
6. C
8. C
10. C

**Page 32**

**Part I**

1. his
2. they
3. her
4. they
5. her

**Part II**

he, she, it, they, you, me, I, us, we

**Page 33**

he—Jack

she—Mandy

it—sunshine

they— Brett, Sadie, and Gage

we—Joan and I

**Page 34**

1. a puppy
2. a tree
3. a baseball glove
4. a computer
5. a cow
6. a piano
7. a television
8. a cupcake
9. a flower
10. a necklace

**Page 35**

1. apples
2. shirts
3. coats
4. movies
5. stars
6. cars
7. trees
8. computers
9. flowers
10. shoes

**Page 36**

Answers will vary

**Page 37**

1. geese
2. stories
3. men
4. oxen
5. leaves
6. berries
7. ladies
8. deer
9. pennies
10. women

**Page 38**

**Common nouns**

1. pizza, supper
2. friend, person
3. cake
4. game
5. sisters
6. bus, students, school
7. teacher, apple
8. teacher, pencil
9. snake, tree
10. day

**Proper nouns**

1. Jennifer, Fridays
2. (none)
3. Joe
4. Mom, Dad
5. Chloe, Kayla Beth
6. (none)
7. Ella
8. Gage
9. Sally
10. Tuesday

**Page 39**

Answers will vary

**Page 40**

Answers will vary

**Page 41**

**Actions verbs:** sit, skip, ran, sing, start, stop, find, tease, laugh, give

# Answer Key *(cont.)*

**Page 42**

**Present tense** (these should be circled)

1. finish
2. carry
3. clean
4. paint
5. walk
6. laugh
7. lift
8. grin
9. talk
10. wrap
11. pick

**Page 43**

Answers will vary

**Page 44**

Answers will vary

**Page 45**

How many (yellow)

4. some
6. few
7. any
8. several

Which ones (blue)

1. these
3. My
10. those

What kind (orange)

1. delicious
2. red
3. favorite, best
4. green
5. fresh
7. shriveled
9. delicious
10. wonderful

**Page 46**

1. early, late
2. outside, inside
3. first, last
4. tomorrow
5. carefully

6.–10. Answers will vary

**Page 47**

1. quickly
2. yesterday
3. now
4. gladly
5. late
6. everywhere
7. slowly
8. today
9. upstairs
10. quietly

**Page 48**

Answers will vary

**Page 49**

Answers will vary

**Page 50**

Capt.

Mrs.

St.

Dr.

Sept.

Tues.

J.C.

F.B.I.

Ms.

Fri.

**Page 51**

Answers will vary.

**Page 52**

1. d
2. j
3. f
4. g
5. h
6. i
7. c
8. a
9. b
10. e

**Page 53**

1. do not
2. is not
3. can not
4. are not
5. does not
6. have not
7. Michele is
8. will not
9. He is
10. did not

# Answer Key *(cont.)*

**Page 54**

1. Emily's candy
2. Chien's DVD
3. Tyrese's backpack
4. Rafael's camera
5. Keysha's necklace
6. Elissa's game
7. Sharon's puzzle
8. Samuel's shoes
9. Aina's book
10. Brody's bike

**Page 55**

Answers will vary

**Page 56**

1. "I can't wait for summer vacation," Ted said.
2. "I can't wait either," Addison agreed.
3. "Where are you going on vacation?" Ted asked.
4. "We're going to Hawaii," Addison said.
5. "That sounds very nice," Ted replied.
6. "Where are you going?" Addison asked.
7. Ted replied, "Well, it's not exactly Hawaii, but there is water there."
8. "Well, where is it?" Addison asked again.
9. "I'm going to spend my vacation working at my Uncle Bob's carwash," Ted finally told her.
10. "I guess you're right. There will be plenty of water," Addison said with a smile.

**Page 57**

Sentences with personification:

2, 3, 5, 7, 8

**Page 58**

Answers will vary

**Page 59**

Answers will vary

**Page 60**

Answers will vary

**Page 61**

Metaphors:

chocolate is a dream

it is gold for the tongue

chocolate is definitely heaven

chocolate is a cartoon character

**Page 62**

**Part I**

Answers will vary

**Part II**

5. H
6. X
7. H
8. X

**Page 63**

Answers will vary

**Page 64**

Answers will vary

**Page 65**

1. E
2. A
3. B
4. C
5. D

6.–10. Answers will vary

**Page 66**

Answers will vary

**Page 67**

1. 8
2. 8
3. 10
4. 8
5. 7
6. 9
7. 9
8. 9
9. 6
10. 9
11. 6
12. 10
13. 8
14. 7
15. 8

**Page 68**

1. 11
2. 15
3. 10
4. 7
5. 11
6. 11
7. 4

# Answer Key *(cont.)*

8. 8
9. 17
10. 13

**Page 69**

1. D
2. A
3. B
4. D
5. B

**Page 70**

1. 3
2. 4
3. 5
4. 0
5. 0
6. 8
7. 10
8. 9
9. 9
10. 4

**Page 71**

1. 40
2. 50
3. 101
4. 32
5. 32
6. 40
7. 81
8. 100
9. 80
10. 71
11. 71
12. 90
13. 31
14. 82
15. 42
16. 32
17. 22
18. 31
19. 64
20. 36
21. 83

**Page 72**

1. 517
2. 350
3. 781
4. 230
5. 902
6. 441
7. 861
8. 770
9. 781
10. 869 pennies
11. 349 days
12. 922 cards

**Page 73**

1. 67
2. 99
3. 111
4. 87
5. 95
6. 110
7. 90
8. 107
9. 116
10. 48
11. 102
12. 90
13. 75
14. 43
15. 114
16. 99
17. 96
18. 110
19. 95

**Page 74**

1. 21.34
2. 28.90
3. 99.22
4. 22.04
5. 29.6
6. 16.8
7. 74.6
8. 8.1
9. 11.09
10. 11.20
11. 40.5
12. 34.00

# Answer Key *(cont.)*

13. 13.42
14. 47.89
15. 99.23
16. 33.33
17. 96.65
18. 111.10

**Page 75**

1. 3
2. 5
3. 7
4. 1
5. 1
6. 2
7. 2
8. 0
9. 4
10. 3
11. 6
12. 3
13. 3
14. 2
15. 4
16. 3
17. 3
18. 0
19. 3
20. 5

**Page 76**

1. 74
2. 11
3. 57
4. 47
5. 65
6. 7
7. 69
8. 28
9. 66
10. 50
11. 13
12. 1
13. 2
14. 10
15. 10

16.–19. Answers will vary

**Page 77**

1. 28
2. 9
3. 20
4. 43
5. 57
6. 500
7. 356
8. 42
9. 50
10. 12
11. 33
12. 55
13. 31
14. 31
15. 58
16. 27
17. 45
18. 15
19. 10
20. 33
21. 10
22. 45

**Page 77**

1. 619
2. 111
3. 289
4. 23
5. 110
6. 218
7. 10
8. 90
9. 348
10. 369
11. 0
12. 591
13. 728
14. 10
15. 61

**Page 78**

1. 619
2. 111
3. 289

# Answer Key *(cont.)*

4. 23
5. 110
6. 218
7. 10
8. 90
9. 348
10. 369
11. 0
12. 591
13. 728
14. 10
15. 61
16. 346
17. 203
18. 173
19. 100
20. 100
21. 12
22. 74
23. 386
24. 307

**Page 79**

1. 212
2. 432
3. 427
4. 440
5. 191
6. 120
7. 362
8. 239
9. 214
10. 355
11. 65
12. 93
13. 73
14. 10
15. 35

**Page 80**

1. 15 students
2. 26 turtles
3. 250 candy bars
4. 31 lemonade products
5. 767 acorns

**Page 81**

1. 16
2. 25
3. 18
4. 12
5. 16
6. 7
7. 9
8. 28

**Page 82**

1. 3
2. 4
3. 6
4. 9
5. 21
6. 16
7. 6
8. 10
9. 18
10. 24

**Page 83**

1. 16
2. 25
3. 36
4. 0
5. 0
6. 0
7. 12
8. 15
9. 18
10. 28
11. 35
12. 42
13. 40
14. 50
15. 60
16. 32
17. 40
18. 48
19. 8
20. 10
21. 12

# Answer Key *(cont.)*

22. 20
23. 25
24. 30
25. 36
26. 45
27. 54
28. 48
29. 60
30. 72

**Page 84**

1. 7
2. 56
3. 21
4. 54
5. 0
6. 42
7. 24
8. 14
9. 72
10. 28
11. 18
12. 56
13. 27
14. 35
15. 48
16. 90
17. 96
18. 99
19. 64
20. 49

**Page 85**

1. 100
2. 66
3. 60
4. 40
5. 88
6. 84
7. 20
8. 33
9. 144
10. 110
11. 11
12. 48
13. 60
14. 66
15. 24
16. 121
17. 100
18. 12

**Page 86**

1. 4
2. 120
3. 28
4. 16
5. 27
6. 63
7. 0
8. 45
9. 72
10. 132
11. 21
12. 18
13. 30
14. 16
15. 81

**Page 87**

Students should circle two equal groups and leave remainders for each problem.

**Page 88**

1. 9
2. 5
3. 12
4. 4
5. 8
6. 10
7. 3
8. 7
9. 11
10. 3
11. 4
12. 8
13. 6
14. 7
15. 5
16. 2
17. 9
18. 11
19. 2
20. 3
21. 3

# Answer Key *(cont.)*

22. 2
23. 2
24. 2

**Page 89**

1. X
2. Color
3. Color
4. X
5. Color
6. Color
7. X
8. Color
9. Color
10. X
11. Color
12. X
13. Color
14. Color
15. X

**Page 90**

1. 3
2. 2
3. 9
4. 5
5. 7
6. 12
7. 1
8. 4
9. 11
10. 6
11. 8

You are smart!

**Page 91**

1. b
2. a
3. c
4. c
5. c
6. b
7. a
8. c
9. b
10. c
11. a
12. c
13. c
14. b

**Page 92**

1. 9, 27
2. 3, 12
3. 3, 18
4. 5, 10
5. 8, 88
6. 5, 45
7. 7, 7
8. 7, 28
9. 12, 36
10. 6, 60
11. 11, 44
12. 4, 24
13. 10, 50
14. 7, 56
15. 7, 14
16. 12, 48

**Page 93**

1. c
2. b
3. a
4. c
5. d
6. a
7. a
8. c

**Page 94**

1. 5
2. 10
3. 10
4. 5
5. 20
6. 20
7. 10
8. 10
9. 5
10. 3
11. 10
12. 8
13. 700
14. 10

# Answer Key *(cont.)*

15. 10
16. 80
17. 5
18. 2
19. 40
20. 10

**Page 95**

1. 2, 20, 200, 2,000
2. 3, 30, 300, 3,000
3. 4, 40, 400, 4,000
4. 6, 60, 600, 6,000
5. 5, 50, 500, 5,000
6. 3, 30, 300, 3,000
7. 1, 10, 100, 1,000
8. 4, 40, 400, 4,000
9. 2, 20, 200, 2,000
10. 2, 20, 200, 2,000

**Page 96**

1. 36 r1
2. 18 r3
3. 12 r1
4. 10 r8
5. 13 r2
6. 10 r2
7. 19 r3
8. 28 r1
9. 14 r1
10. 3 r3
11. 27 r1
12. 12 r1
13. 18 r1
14. 2 r3
15. 24 r1
16. 2 r3
17. 12 r2
18. 14 r4
19. 12 r1
20. 7
21. 44 pieces, yes

**Page 97**

1. b
2. a
3. c
4. e
5. f
6. d

7.–10. Drawings will vary

**Page 98**

1. 3/10
2. 3/6
3. 5/6
4. 7/8
5. 5/7
6. 2/3
7. 4/7
8. 1/2

**Page 99**

1. 5/5
2. 5/8
3. 2/3
4. 5/6
5. 4/4
6. 7/10
7. 3/8
8. 3/6
9. 4/10
10. 1/4
11. 1/3
12. 2/9
13. 3/3
14. 1/6

**Page 100**

1. c
2. b
3. a
4. c

**Page 101**

***Part I***

1. j
2. a
3. h
4. i
5. g
6. b
7. c
8. e
9. f
10. d

# Answer Key *(cont.)*

***Part II***

11. 13 x 13, 14 x 14, 15 x 15
12. JKL, MNO, PQR
13. 4444, 55555, 666666
14. 70, 85, 100
15. 1/7, 1/8, 1/9

**Page 102**

1. 8 square units
2. 10 square units
3. 6 square units
4. 5 square units
5. 3 square units
6. 4 square units

7.–12. Answers will vary.

**Page 103**

No key needed.

**Page 104**

Answers will vary

**Page 105**

1. 7 cm
2. 1 dm
3. 5 cm

**Page 106**

1. b
2. a
3. b
4. a
5. b
6. a
7. b
8. a
9. a
10. a

**Page 107**

Answers will vary.

**Page 108**

1. cone
2. cubes
3. rectangular prism
4. rectangular prism
5. sphere
6. cone
7. cylinder
8. cubes
9. cylinder
10. sphere

**Page 109**

Answers will vary

**Page 110**

1. a
2. c
3. c
4. b

5.–7. Answers will vary.

**Page 111**

1.–6. Answers will vary.

7. yes
8. no
9. no
10. yes
11. yes
12. yes

**Page 112**

Answers will vary

**Page 113**

Answers will vary

**Page 114**

1. 

2. 

3.

4. 

5. 

**Page 115**

Answers will vary

**Page 116**

1. 5:15
2. 9:30
3. 6:15
4. 10:30
5. 6:30
6. 11:15
7. 7:00
8. 4:15
9. 10:00
10. 3:30
11. 5:30
12. 12:00
13. 1:15
14. 2:30
15. 3:00

 

# Answer Key *(cont.)*

16. 7:30
17. 8:00
18. 1:00
19. 2:00
20. 9:15
21. 4:00

**Page 117**

***Part I***

1. 7:30
2. 8:15
3. 9:00
4. 5:15
5. 12:00

**Page 118**

1. 2 hours
2. 1 hour
3. 3:45
4. 3 hours
5. 2:45
6. 2 hours

**Page 119**

1. 16¢ or $.16
2. 95¢ or $.95
3. 83¢ or $.83
4. 35¢ or $.35
5. 50¢ or $.50
6. 70¢ or $.70
7. 87¢ or $.87
8. 80¢ or $.80
9. 75¢ or $.75

**Page 120**

1. $3.40 — yes
2. $4.75
3. 10¢
4. 32¢

**Page 121**

1. $10.05
2. $11.20
3. $.98
4. $4.80
5. 3.30
6. $1.13
7. $8.00
8. $.39
9. $.86
10. $2.80

**Page 122**

1. 2 1/2 hours
2. 1 hour
3. reading class, because it is 2 hours long and music is only 1 hour
4. art class
5. math class
6. lunch

**Page 123**

Answers will vary.

**Page 124**

1. blue jays and robins
2. mockingbirds
3. 15 blue jays
4. 20 total
5. 55 birds

**Page 125**

1. Toronto
2. 15 students
3. Myrtle Beach and Vancouver
4. 9 votes each
5. Cancun
6. 6 votes
7. 9 votes
8. 51 total votes

**Page 126**

Answers will vary.

**Page 127**

1. False
2. True
3. False
4. True
5. False
6. 4
7. 1
8. 2
9. 3

**Page 128**

environment

adapt

desert

water

food

# Answer Key *(cont.)*

sunlight

living

weather

protection

**Page 129**

***Part II***

1. flower
2. stem
3. roots
4. leaf
5. flower
6. roots

**Page 130**

1. i
2. a
3. b
4. g
5. h
6. j
7. c
8. f
9. e
10. d

**Page 131**

Answers will vary.

**Page 132**

***Part I***

1. I
2. L
3. I
4. I
5. L
6. I
7. L
8. I
9. L
10. L

***Part II***

Answers will vary.

**Page 133**

1. o
2. h
3. h
4. c
5. c
6. h
7. h
8. h
9. h
10. h

**Page 134**

1. f
2. e
3. h
4. g
5. b
6. c
7. d
8. a

9.–16. Answers will vary.

**Page 135**

1. b
2. a
3. b
4. b
5. a
6. a
7. b
8. a

**Page 136**

Answers will vary.

**Page 137**

Answers will vary.

**Page 138**

Answers will vary.

**Page 139**

Rocks that should have an X:

1, 4, 7, 9, and 10

**Page 140**

Answers will vary.

**Page 141**

1. e
2. a
3. d
4. b
5. c

**Page 142**

Answers that should be colored:

1, 3, 4, 5, 7

**Page 143**

1. evaporation
2. condensation
3. precipitation
4. runoff
5. 4

# Answer Key *(cont.)*

6. vapor
7. precipitation
8. (any 3) rain, snow, hail, sleet

9–10 Answers will vary.

**Page 144**

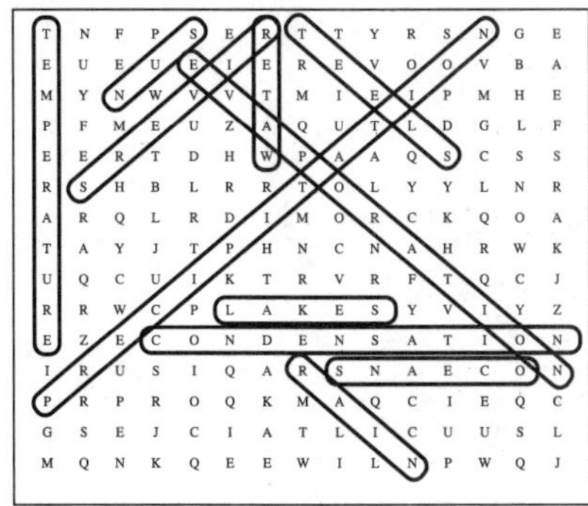

**Page 145**

***Part I***

Answers will vary.

***Part II***

7. 24 hours
8. whether a part of the Earth is turned towards or away from the sun
9. sun
10. away

**Page 146**

1. sunshine
2. moon
3. moon
4. sunshine
5. sunshine
6. moon

**Page 147**

1. a
2. a
3. b
4. b
5. a

**Page 148**

New moon, first quarter moon, full moon, last quarter moon

**Page 149**

***Part I***

Mercury, Venus, Earth, Mars, Jupiter, Saturn, Uranus, Neptune, Pluto

***Part II***

Answers will vary.

**Page 150**

***Part II***

1. Mercury
2. Venus
3. Earth
4. Mars
5. Sun
6. Earth

**Page 151**

***Part II***

1. e
2. c
3. d
4. b
5. a

**Page 152**

Answers will vary.

**Page 153**

Statements that should be colored:

2, 3, 5, 8, 9, 10, 11

**Page 154**

1. pull
2. push
3. pull
3. pull
4. push
5. push
6. push
7. push
8. push
9. push
10. pull
11. pull/push
12. pull

**Page 155**

1. a
2. b
3. b
4. a
5. b

**Page 156**

Objects that should be circled:

a nail, a paper clip, a metal washer, a metal fork, a metal bolt, another magnet

# Answer Key *(cont.)*

## Page 157

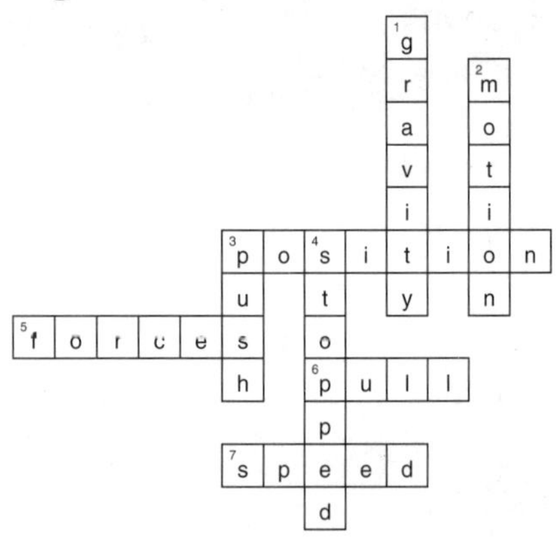

## Page 158

1. liquid
2. gas
3. solid
4. liquid
5. gas
6. solid
7. solid
8. liquid
9. gas
10. liquid
11. liquid
12. solid
13. liquid
14. gas
15. solid

## Page 159

Answers will vary.

## Page 160

Objects that should be circled: rock, computer, elephant, tree, watermelon, grown woman, ape, car, jug, gallon of ice cream, lamp, keychain, grown dog, camera, bowling ball, baseball bat, boot, pair of scissors, book, eagle

## Page 161

1. properties
2. size, color, and shape
3. gas
4. liquid
5. solid
6. mass
7. weight
8. particles

## Page 162

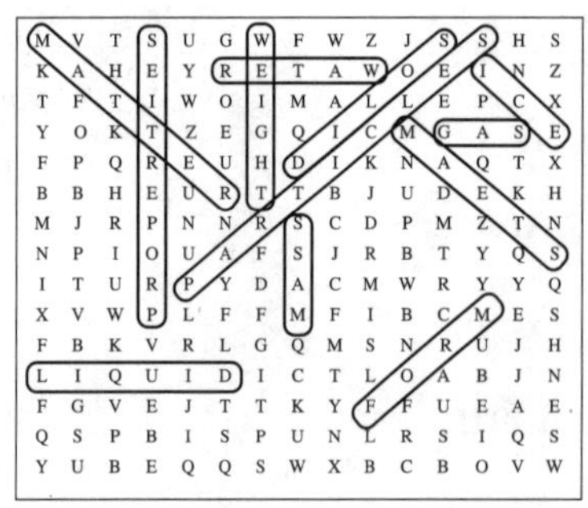